MW00898196

The 40-Week Ironman

Copyright © 2023 by Matt Carufel. All rights reserved.

Independently Published, and printed by Kindle Direct Publishing in the USA.

No part of this book may be reproduced or used in any manner without the prior written permission of the copyright owner, except for the use of brief quotations in a book review.

Limit of Liability/Disclaimer of Warranty: While the publisher and the author have used their best efforts in preparing this book, they make no representations or warranties with respect to the accuracy or completeness of the contents of this book and specifically disclaim any implied warranties of merchantability or fitness for a particular purpose. No warranty may be created or extended by sales representatives or written sales materials. The advice and strategies contained herein may not be suitable for your situation. This book does not replace the advice of a medical professional. No information presented herein should be construed as medical advice. Readers should consult a physician and obtain permission before starting any new exercise program or diet.

For general information on our other products and services or for technical support, please contact us at hi@swimbikerun101.com.

ISBN: 9798394386015 (Paperback)

S swimbikerun101.com

Dedications: SNC, MMC, and ABC, through fits and starts, pandemic, and injury the vision of holding you all at the finish line picked me up each time I fell. I love you with my whole rainbow heart.

You're holding a field guide for Ironman training. All the information you need – when you need it, so you can start right now, and train with confidence.

The 40-Week Ironman

s swimbikerun101.com

Written & Designed by
Matthew J. Carufel

THIS BOOK WILL HELP YOU...

Find Your Motivation

We'll help you break down your motivation into its fundamental essence, then we'll help you enrich it into a powerful, emotionally evocative vision that will be the thrust behind you on your journey to become an Ironman finisher.

Start strong

Getting started can be a major hurdle; we'll walk you through the process, so you can start quickly and with confidence.

Gear Up

Triathlon, in general, and Ironman – specifically – requires a *lot* of gear, and as a newcomer to the sport it can be hard to know what's critical. We'll help you figure out what gear you need, and when you need to get it, so you can focus on training.

Swim with Confidence

We'll help you overcome the mental and physical barriers keeping you from feeling confident in open water.

Pace Yourself

Get to the finish line without burnout with prescribed levels of effort for each workout, and a proven balance of training to recovery in each training phase.

Tailor Each Workout

Week-by-week, workout-by-workout, we'll lay out a proven roadmap for getting from wherever you're at today to the finish line.

Master The Important Details

You'll get in-depth training on the most important aspects of Ironman training: nutrition, transitions, and logistics to name just a few.

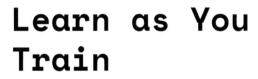

Learn as You Train

We won't keep you in the dark, or swamp you with information you don't need. We'll give you what you need to know - when you need to know it.

We've curated hard-won advice, tips, tricks, and coaching advice that we'll feed to you throughout the duration of the 40-week program.

Use Food as Fuel

Nutrition is commonly referred to as "the fourth discipline of Ironman." We'll help you develop a customized, science-based fueling plan so you can master your race nutrition.

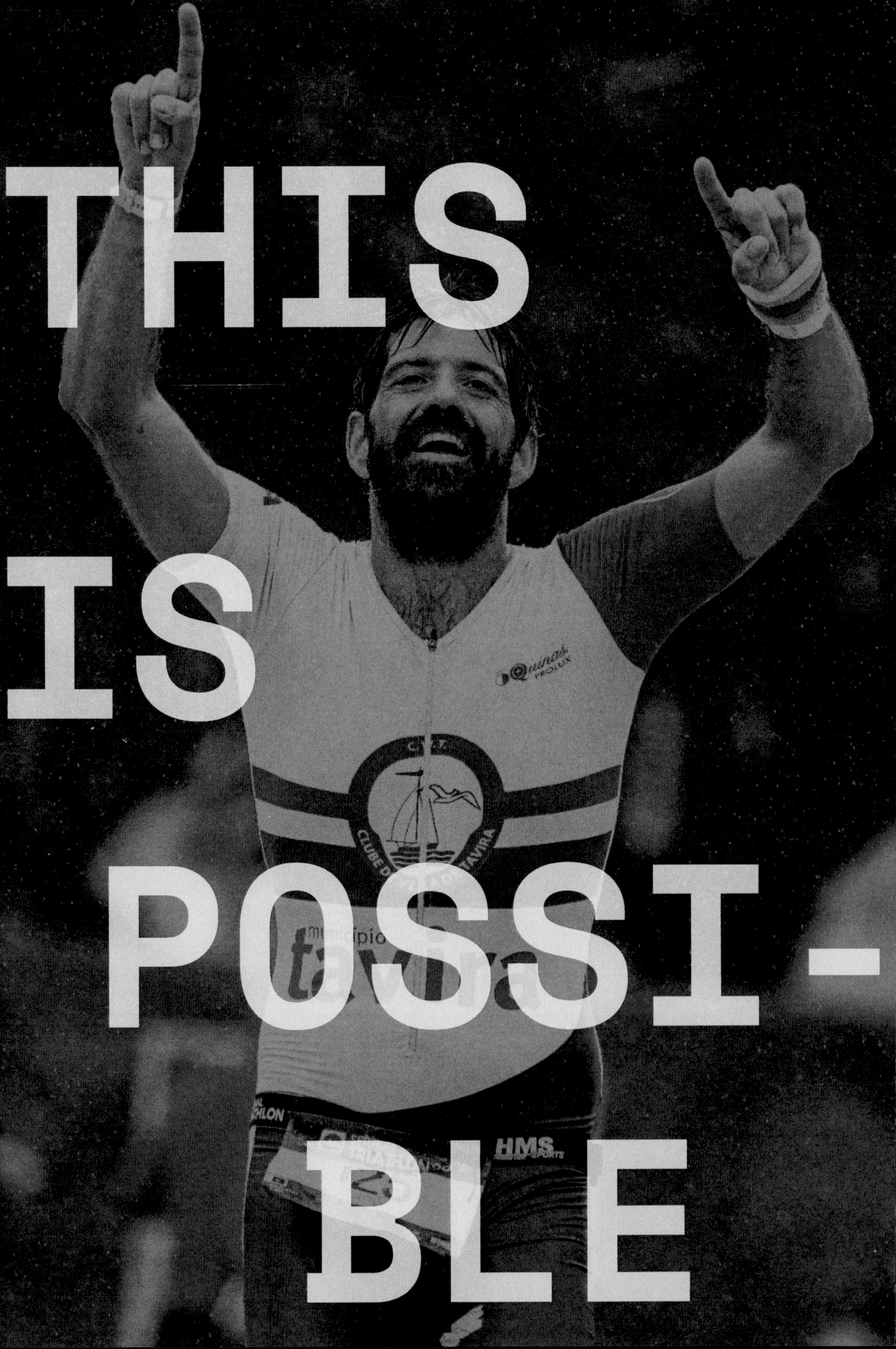
THIS
IS
POSSI-
BLE
Quinas
PROLUX
município
tavira
HMS

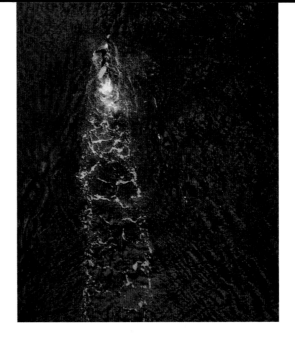

When I signed up for my first Ironman, I was in deep water. I was buoyant at best, didn't own a bike, and had only run a 5K race prior. I didn't know what to do, or where to look for help, so I scoured for the best books, but they left me more confused than when I started.

So I took matters into my own hands and wrote this book, an easy-to-use resource for triathlon rookies like I once was. This book is a no-frills, step-by-step guide to take you from zero to Ironman in just 40 weeks.

No need to read hundreds of pages or have any prior knowledge. Just follow along page-by-page, and mile-by-mile, and you'll be spoon-fed everything you need to know – when you need to know it. By the end, you'll be a full-fledged Ironman. Let's do this.

THE PLAN

5 distinct phases of training:

20 ACCLIMATION
Get started, establish your Ironman routine, and build good habits

31 BASE PHASE
Introduce open-water swimming and "brick workouts"

60 BUILD PHASE
Ramp bike and run volume, and begin to practice nutrition

71 PEAK PHASE
Maximum training volumes at race intensity

79 TAPER
Significant reduction of volume to allow time for recovery

CONTENTS

START HERE

For most who are new to the sport, figuring out how to even get started can be a significant hurdle. Here's how:

1. Assess where you're at - this plan takes athletes from running about 10mi/week and biking about 20mi/wk. to competition-ready in 40 weeks.

If you're not able to complete that kind of running and biking volume today, that's fine, but you'll need to factor in additional time on top of the 40 weeks to build to the point that you're ready to start this plan.

Wherever you're at, you should be able to add about one mile of total running, and 4mi of total biking to your weekly training volume each week to build to the point that you can start this plan.

For example: if you are only running about 3 miles per week today, you should be able to safely run 4 total miles next week, then five the following, and so on.

Same concept for biking, but increasing weekly total bike volume by four miles: do 5mi this week, 9 next week, and so on.

What about swimming, you ask? No matter where you're at with swimming – including having zero swimming experience – you will be able to pick up and start this program.

If you're totally new to swimming, don't get discouraged. Many triathletes – self included – started from scratch with swimming.

Don't worry if you can't do 1,000 yards of total swimming out of the gate. Do what you can handle, focus on building good form, and you'll catch up with the planned volumes – you'll get there. Promise.

2. Pick a race - assuming you're starting from scratch, you'll want to find a race that is scheduled for about one year from today, to leave time to gather the needed gear (more on that later) to start training.

Pick a race location nearby where you live; it'll cut down on expenses, and logistics challenges. When you find the race you want; buy a spot.

At the same time, you'll also want to book your hotel (the ones closest to the race will book quickly, and prices will only go up as you draw closer to the race).

3. Get needed training gear - No sugarcoating it; there's a lot of gear needed to train for an Ironman.

We cut out the noise with our essential tri training gear on page 13 to help you focus on getting the absolute must-have gear.

Once you've got a race booked, the gear you'll need for training, and the physical ability to begin this plan, you're ready to jump in.

4. Align Training Plan to Your Race - No need to wait on getting started with your own training; by all means – start building your ability now, but it'll be important to align this program to the race date to make sure you're doing the right training at the right time.

To do that, begin week 1 programming 39 weeks prior to the week of your race.

The last piece, "why" is so important it gets its own section.

07

"You don't have to be great to start,
but you have to start to be great."

Zig Ziglar

Normal people don't *just decide* to be an Ironman.

There's a something special that brought you here.

Whatever that thing is, you're going to have to figure out how to harness it, enrich it, and wield a weapons-grade version of it – against yourself.

Because in the not-too-distant future, self-sabotaging versions of you will come to stand in the way of what you're attempting here.

They'll say "I can just skip my workout today. I'll make it up next week." They'll ask "why am I even doing this?"

In those moments you'll need to be able to come back to the powerful emotions that led you to this point in the first place.

So let's start with the big questions:

Why are you here?

Most people will answer initially with something like "I want to achieve something monumental" or "My friends are doing it; I'm in it for the camaraderie."

That's a first-layer-why answer. Your real motivation for doing this race is the answer you give yourself after asking yourself "why?" five times – a fifth-layer why answer.

Here's how that internal dialog might sound:

1st Layer: Alright, why am I doing an Ironman?

You've always loved a challenge; this is one of the most challenging athletic events out there.

2nd Layer: Okay, but why is it important to me to take on a big challenge like this?

Maybe it's because you like to push yourself beyond your limits and see what you're truly capable of.

3rd Layer: But why is it so important to me to see what I'm capable of?

I think you feel like you need to prove to yourself and others that you can achieve great things.

4th Layer: Why is it so important for me to prove that to myself and others?

I've had doubts in the past about my abilities, and I want to overcome those doubts and feel a sense of accomplishment.

5th Layer: But why do I have those doubts in the first place?

I want to prove to myself that I'm strong and capable because I've felt weak and incapable ever since I lost my job.

Conjuring Your Vision.

Once you've figured out your "why," it's time to turn your attention to the outcomes you're after.

What does it look like to cross the finish line? How will it feel to achieve such a monumental goal after months of toil, dedication, and sacrifice? What kind of person will you become through this experience?

Close your eyes and **imagine yourself in vivid and complete detail in that moment.**

Feel the sun on your face. Hear the waves lapping the shore. See your feet caked with sand still damp with morning dew. Hear the dull clang of the cowbells, and the thunder of the crowd as you round the final corner of the run and approach the finish line. Feel the tears welling in your eyes; as you see – through blurred vision

the final 100 yards of the race. Feel the gripping, finish-line embrace from loved ones, beaming at you in admiration.

This is your vision.

The feeling it gives you is what you'll need to conjure in order to push through the inevitable times when you'll feel like giving up.

You need to hold onto this vision, make it a part of your daily life, and constantly remind yourself why you're doing this.

You've gotta become so deeply emotionally connected to it such that you feel it in your bones, in your heart, in your soul.

Maybe you create a vision board with pictures of the finish line, motivational quotes, and images that inspire you. Maybe you find it embodied in the lyrics of a song. Maybe you write down your vision and read it every day, reminding yourself of why you're doing this and what it means to you.

Whatever makes the vision visceral, and emotional to you – run with that.

That is your special something.

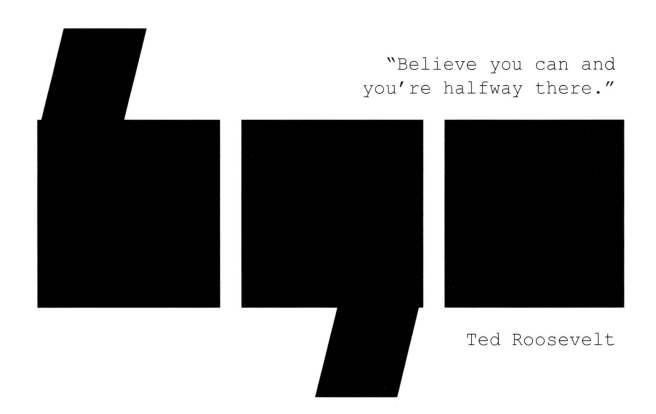

"Believe you can and
you're halfway there."

Ted Roosevelt

N I THINK I CAN

I'm doing an Ironman because...

_____
_____
_____
_____
_____
_____
_____
_____
_____
_____

To keep myself motivated, I'll envision...

_____
_____
_____
_____
_____
_____
_____
_____
_____
_____
_____
_____
_____
_____
_____
_____
_____
_____

SWIM

Gear You Need (and nothing more)

The single most-common question we get from new triathletes is "what do I need to start training?"

This quick start checklist will help you focus on the most important tools you'll need to get started training.

GOGGLES

you'll be wearing these for long periods of time, so make sure they ~~don't hurt~~ are actually really comfortable, and that you'll be able to see long distances (1-200 yards) with them on.

SWIMSUIT

Don't break the bank on this piece of equipment. You don't need anything fancy; you just need something to cover your nether regions.

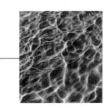

POOL ACCESS

Tough to swim without a pool; not sure where to start? Look for a Masters program near you. You'll get access to a pool, and some solid coaching.

WEEK 1

Make sure you've got a swimsuit (or jammer), goggles, and pool access before week one.

WETSUIT

Sleeves, sleeveless, half-sleeve? These are decisions of personal preference; just make sure you've got one before your first open-water swim.

SWIM BUOY

A potentially life-saving tool designed to (1) make you highly visible to watercraft in the area, and (2) give you a floatation device in the event you need one while swimming in open water.

WEEK 11

Have a wetsuit and swim buoy before week 11.

BIKE

Gear You Need
(and nothing more)

The bike is very "well accessorized" shall we say?

Unlike the swim, you'll need pretty much all of these accessories to get started training for the bike on week one of the plan.

BIKE

You can get by with other frame styles if it's your first race, but you really want a road or tri bike. If you're buying a new bike, get a road bike and don't sacrifice on fit; find a local bike shop, call ahead, and ask them to help you get "sized."

HELMET

An aero helmet will help you look the part of a salty veteran triathlete, but it's absolutely not needed; a road bike helmet will work just fine, and will cost hundreds less.

CYCLING SHOES

Cycling shoes help you make more efficient pedal strokes, creating better power transfer by keeping your feet attached to the bike. A basic pair works just fine; don't get a top-of-the line pair.

PEDALS

Attach your shoe (and foot) to the bike crank, to make each pedal stroke as efficient and powerful as it can be. Buy them at a local shop and save the headache of trying to attach them yourself.

WEEK 1
Sorry to break it to you, but you need all of this (and more – see next page) before you get started.

SHORTS OR BIBS

Either will have a padded seat area, called a "chamois pad," that keeps your bottom from getting sore. Bibs are great for the kind of people that would be bothered by a waistband pinching your their midsection.

JERSEY

Pick one that's tight-fitting (to eliminate drag) and high-visibility (for on-road safety).

SUNGLASSES

They're going to get broken, dirty, scratched or lost; just buy a cheap pair with interchangeable lenses so you can wear them in any light condition.

WATER BOTTLES

You'll lose a few; get six, and buy cheap, BPA-free ones.

SAFETY LIGHTS

Be seen; stay alive -- never leave home for a bike ride without them.

TIRE PUMP

You'll use it before each ride to top off your tires. Don't buy the cheapest one you can find; they tend to be a frustrating experience, we've found.

WEEK 1
Make sure you've got all of these ready before your first ride.

Need More Gear Help?

Or just looking for a reasonable perspective on other, non-essential triathlon gear?

We maintain a gear guide on our website to help triathletes make sense of a comprehensive list of gear, tools, accessories, and apps – essential or otherwise..

Gear guide

RUN

Gear You Need
(and nothing more)

Don't take the shoe-buying decision lightly. No equipment purchase matters more than this one.

Get help from a trusted, local running store; they'll help you find a shoe that fits your foot, and your running style.

SHOES

Like a bike, fit really matters here. Find a local running shop with a good reputation for helping runners find a well-fitting shoe, and have them help you find a match for your foot and stride

SHORTS

Maybe you're a pants person – we don't know; Just make sure you've got something lightweight, breathable, and designed for running.

TOPS

Moisture-wicking and breathable tops designed for running in the range of temperatures you'll see in your local climate.

SUNGLASSES

Use the same, cheap pair you'll wear on your bike.

RUNNING HAT

Lightweight and breathable – keep the sun off your face and head.

WEEK 1
First run workout.

Each of our bike and run workouts will specify a Rating of Perceived Exertion Zone (RPEZ) that you should use to guide your level of effort throughout the prescribed workouts in this plan.

Those zones are defined by how hard – or easy – each level of exertion feels to you subjectively:

RPEZ

What is Perceived Exertion?

10 ALL OUT

You're completely out of breath, unable to talk. And can only maintain the effort for short bursts.

9 VERY HARD

Difficult to maintain intensity. Can barely breathe and can only speak a few words

7-8 VIGOROUS

Borderline uncomfortable. Short of breath, can speak a sentence before breaking to catch your breath.

4-6 MODERATE

Breathing heavily, but can hold a short conversation. Still somewhat comfortable, but becoming noticeably more challenging

2-3 LIGHT

Feels like you can maintain for hours. Easy to breathe and carry on a conversation

1 VERY LIGHT

Hardly any exertion, but more than sleeping or watching TV, etc.

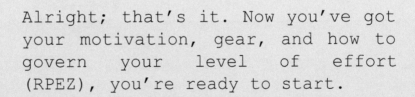

Alright; that's it. Now you've got your motivation, gear, and how to govern your level of effort (RPEZ), you're ready to start.

Jump into week one training, and we'll feed you the information you need – as you need it.

Up first: The Acclimation phase of training. The purpose of this 10-week phase is to help you and your body become accustomed to the new training load and routine while gradually building fitness.

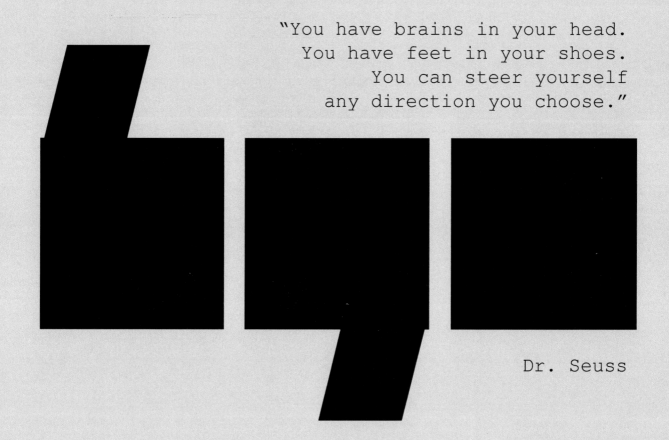

"You have brains in your head.
You have feet in your shoes.
You can steer yourself
any direction you choose."

Dr. Seuss

Week 1

Acclimation

Important Notes:

- ☐ Before you start, make sure you've got the essential training equipment (see pg. 13)
- ☐ Not able to finish these distances yet? Not a problem. Start from distances you can maintain without going above RPEZ 8, and add 1 mile/week to your run, or 4 miles/week to your bike training volume until you can do these distances comfortably.

M	Tu	W	Th	F	Sa	Su
Rest	S - 1,000 W - BWC	B - 7 mi.	S - 1,200 W - DLC	R - 3 mi.	B - 13 mi.	R - 4 mi.

Bike (B)

7 miles
Warmup
• 2 mi @ RPEZ 3-4
Workout
• 4 mi @ RPEZ 6-7
Cooldown
• 1 mi @ RPEZ 2

13 miles
Warmup
• 2 mi @ RPEZ 2-3
Workout
• 10 mi @ RPEZ 4-5
Cooldown
• 1 mi @ RPEZ 2

Run (R)

3 miles
Warmup
• 0.5 mi @ RPEZ 2-3
Workout
• 2.25 mi @ RPEZ 5-6
Cooldown
• 0.25 mi @ RPEZ 2

4 miles
Warmup
• 0.5 mi @ RPEZ 2-3
Workout
• 3.25 mi @ RPEZ 4-5
Cooldown
• 0.25 mi @ RPEZ 2

Week 2

Acclimation

Find a Club

Important Notes:

- ☐ Pro tip: epsom salt baths are great for a sore body; give it a try if you're feeling beat up after week one
- ☐ Swimming with a Masters club will help get you quality coaching on your stroke, and can put a little added social pressure to drive accountability - <u>click</u> to find one near you.

M	Tu	W	Th	F	Sa	Su
Rest	S - 1,250 W - PC	B - 8 mi.	S - 1,300 W - SBC	R - 3 mi.	B - 16 mi.	R - 5 mi

Bike (B)

8 miles
Warmup
• 1 mi @ RPEZ 3-4
Workout
• 6 mi @ RPEZ 6-7
Cooldown
• 1 mi @ RPEZ 2

16 miles
Warmup
• 2 mi @ RPEZ 2-3
Workout
• 13 mi @ RPEZ 4-5
Cooldown
• 1 mi @ RPEZ 2

Run (R)

3 miles
Warmup
• 0.5 mi @ RPEZ 2-3
Workout
• 2 mi @ RPEZ 5-6
Cooldown
• 0.5 mi @ RPEZ 2

5 miles
Warmup
• 0.5 mi @ RPEZ 2-3
Workout
• 4 mi @ RPEZ 4-5
Cooldown
• 0.5 mi @ RPEZ 2

MySwimPro
App

Important Notes:

☐ If you've got a smart watch, download the MySwimPro App to track your swim workouts and highlight progress you make throughout your training.

☐ Most new triathletes find the swim to be the most challenging discipline – at first – by the time you're done, it'll be a cakewalk; just stick with it, and focus on long, smooth strokes.

M	Tu	W	Th	F	Sa	Su
Rest	S - 1,300 W - KBC	B - 9 mi.	S - 1,300 W - RC	R - 2 mi.	B - 19 mi.	R - 5 mi.

Bike (B)

9 miles
Warmup
• 2 mi @ RPEZ 3-4
Workout
• 6 mi @ RPEZ 6-7
Cooldown
• 1 mi @ RPEZ 2

19 miles
Warmup
• 2 mi @ RPEZ 2-3
Workout
• 16 mi @ RPEZ 4-5
Cooldown
• 1 mi @ RPEZ 2

Run (R)

2 miles
Warmup
• 0.5 mi @ RPEZ 2-3
Workout
• 1.25 mi @ RPEZ 5-6
Cooldown
• 0.25 mi @ RPEZ 2

5 miles
Warmup
• 0.5 mi @ RPEZ 2-3
Workout
• 4.25 mi @ RPEZ 4-5
Cooldown
• 0.25 mi @ RPEZ 2

Week 4
Acclimation

Strava App

Important Notes:

- ☐ Check out the <u>Strava App</u>; it can give added motivation to track & share your progress
- ☐ Swimming is *very* counterintuitive: swimming fast feels like long, smooth strokes; talk to your Masters swim coach, or if you're swimming on your own, see if someone will video your freestyle stroke so you can start to develop awareness of your stroke mechanics

M	Tu	W	Th	F	Sa	Su
Rest	S - 1,300 W - BWC	B - 9 mi.	S - 1,400 W - DLC	R - 4 mi.	B - 17 mi.	R - 5 mi

Bike (B)

9 miles
Warmup
- 2 mi @ RPEZ 3-4
Workout
{Repeat 2x}
- 2 mi @ RPEZ 5-6
- 1 mi @ RPEZ 7-8
Cooldown
- 1 mi @ RPEZ 2

17 miles
Warmup
- 2 mi @ RPEZ 2-3
Workout
- 14 mi @ RPEZ 4-5
Cooldown
- 1 mi @ RPEZ 2

Run (R)

4 miles
Warmup
- 0.5 mi @ RPEZ 2-3
Workout
{Repeat 3x}
- 0.25 mi @ RPEZ 7-8
- 0.75 mi @ RPEZ 4-5
Cooldown
- 0.5 mi @ RPEZ 2

5 miles
Warmup
- 0.5 mi @ RPEZ 2-3
Workout
- 4.25 mi @ RPEZ 4-5
Cooldown
- 0.25 mi @ RPEZ 2

Swim (S)

1,300 yds.
Warmup
- 1x100 freestyle
- 1x100 pull
- 1x100 kick

Workout
{15 sec rest between each of 10 sets}
- 6x50 freestyle
- 3x100 pull
- 2x100 kick
- 4x50 freestyle down, choice back

Cooldown
- 1x50 freestyle
- 1x50 choice

1,400 yds.
Warmup
- 1x100 freestyle
- 1x100 pull
- 1x100 kick

Workout
{15 sec rest between each of 14 sets}
- 4x100 freestyle
- 1x100 pull
- 2x50 kick
- 6x50 freestyle down, choice back

Cooldown
- 1x50 freestyle
- 1x50 choice

Weights (W)

Bodyweight Circuit (BWC)
Repeat 3-4x
- 10 squats
- 20 single-leg lunges (10 each)
- 10 push-ups
- 20 mountain climbers
- 10 plank jacks
- Rest 1 min

Dumbbell Leg Circuit (DLC)
Repeat 3-4x
- 10 dumbbell squats
- 10 dumbbell deadlifts
- 10 dumbbell lunges (each leg)
- 10 dumbbell step-ups (each leg)
- 10 calf raises
- Rest for 1 minute

Week 5

Acclimation

Important Notes:

☐ It's too common for new cyclists to have a "cliptastrophy" – falling over while stopped at a red light or stop sign because they forgot to unclip their shoe from their pedal, and aren't able to catch their fall. Unclip as soon as you know you're going to stop to save the embarrassment and road rash.

M	Tu	W	Th	F	Sa	Su
Rest	S - 1,400 W - PC	B - 11 mi.	S - 1,400 W - SBC	R - 3 mi.	B - 22 mi.	R - 6 mi.

Bike (B)

11 miles
Warmup
• 2 mi @ RPEZ 3-4
Workout
• 8 mi @ RPEZ 5-6
Cooldown
• 1 mi @ RPEZ 2

22 miles
Warmup
• 2 mi @ RPEZ 2-3
Workout
• 19 mi @ RPEZ 4-5
Cooldown
• 1 mi @ RPEZ 2

Run (R)

3 miles
Warmup
• 0.5 mi @ RPEZ 2-3
Workout
• 2.25 mi @ RPEZ 5-6
Cooldown
• 0.25 mi @ RPEZ 2

6 miles
Warmup
• 0.5 mi @ RPEZ 2-3
Workout
• 5.25 mi @ RPEZ 4-5
Cooldown
• 0.25 mi @ RPEZ 2

Week 6
Acclimation

Open-water swimming

Important Notes:

- ☐ Our first open-water swim is coming up in 5 weeks; find a good place to swim, and make sure you've got (1) a wetsuit, and (2) an open-water safety buoy, and (3) read this
- ☐ Start to experiment with different fueling options during high-volume workouts to find what works best for you; aim to consume 60g of carbs per hour

M	Tu	W	Th	F	Sa	Su
Rest	S - 1,400 W - KBC	B - 12 mi.	S - 1,400 W - RC	R - 4 mi.	B - 25 mi.	R - 6 mi.

Bike (B)

12 miles
Warmup
• 2 mi @ RPEZ 3-4
Workout
{Repeat 3x}
• 1 mi @ RPEZ 7-8
• 2 mi @ RPEZ 4-5
Cooldown
• 1 mi @ RPEZ 2

25 miles
Warmup
• 2 mi @ RPEZ 2-3
Workout
• 22 mi @ RPEZ 4-5
Cooldown
• 1 mi @ RPEZ 2

Run (R)

4 miles
Warmup
• 0.5 mi @ RPEZ 2-3
Workout
{Repeat 3x}
• 0.25 mi @ RPEZ 8-9
• 0.75 mi @ RPEZ 4-5
Cooldown
• 0.5 mi @ RPEZ 2

6 miles
Warmup
• 0.5 mi @ RPEZ 2-3
Workout
• 5.25 mi @ RPEZ 4-5
Cooldown
• 0.25 mi @ RPEZ 2

Swim (S)

1,400 yds.
Warmup
• 1x100 freestyle
• 4x50 choice
• 4x25 freestyle sprints

Workout

1,450 yds.
Warmup
• 1x100 freestyle
• 1x50 kick
• 1x100 pull

Workout

Weights (W)

Kettlebell Circuit (KBC)
Repeat 3-4x
• 10 kettlebell swings
• 10 goblet squats
• 10 kettlebell lunges (each leg)
• 20 single-arm kettlebell rows
• Rest for 1 minute

Week 7

Acclimation

Bike cadence

Important Notes:

☐ Cycling at a higher cadence improves efficiency and reduces stress on the legs, while cycling at a lower cadence can help build muscle strength and power. Most triathletes prefer a race cadence of 80 - 100 RPM, but you should experiment with cadence to find what feels best to you. Read this for more.

M	Tu	W	Th	F	Sa	Su
Rest	S - 1,500 W - BWC	B - 12 mi.	S - 1,500 W - DLC	R - 3 mi.	B - 28 mi.	R - 7 mi.

Bike (B)

12 miles
Warmup
• 2 mi @ RPEZ 3-4
Workout
• 9 mi @ RPEZ 4-5
Cooldown
• 1 mi @ RPEZ 2

28 miles
Warmup
• 2 mi @ RPEZ 2-3
Workout
• 25 mi @ RPEZ 4-5
Cooldown
• 1 mi @ RPEZ 2

Run (R)

3 miles
Warmup
• 0.5 mi @ RPEZ 2-3
Workout
• 2.25 mi @ RPEZ 5-6
Cooldown
• 0.25 mi @ RPEZ 2

7 miles
Warmup
• 0.5 mi @ RPEZ 2-3
Workout
• 6.25 mi @ RPEZ 4-5
Cooldown
• 0.25 mi @ RPEZ 2

Week 8

Acclimation

Bike fitting 101

Important Notes:

- ☐ Now that you've gotten about 200 miles on your bike, it's a good time to get "fitted." Call your local shop, and ask for help. They'll get you on your bike, and help you make customizations to make you more powerful and comfortable on your bike - read more here.
- ☐ An aero bar is a solid investment; consider adding one at your bike fitting.

M	Tu	W	Th	F	Sa	Su
Rest	S - 1,500 W - PC	B - 11 mi.	S - 1,500 W - SBC	R - 5 mi.	B - 25 mi.	R - 7 mi.

Bike (B)

11 miles
Warmup
- 2 mi @ RPEZ 3-4
Workout
- 8 mi @ RPEZ 4-5
Cooldown
- 1 mi @ RPEZ 2

25 miles
Warmup
- 2 mi @ RPEZ 2-3
Workout
- 22 mi @ RPEZ 4-5
Cooldown
- 1 mi @ RPEZ 2

Run (R)

5 miles
Warmup
- 0.5 mi @ RPEZ 2-3
Workout
- 4.25 mi @ RPEZ 5-6
Cooldown
- 0.25 mi @ RPEZ 2

7 miles
Warmup
- 0.5 mi @ RPEZ 2-3
Workout
- 6.25 mi @ RPEZ 4-5
Cooldown
- 0.25 mi @ RPEZ 2

Swim (S)

1,500 yds.
Warmup
- 2x100 freestyle
- 1x100 pull
- 2x50 kick

Workout

1,500 yds.
Warmup
- 2x100 freestyle
- 1x100 pull
- 2x50 kick

Workout

Weights (W)

Plyometric Circuit (PC)
Repeat 4x
- 10 box jumps
- 10 jump squats
- 10 jump lunges (each leg)
- 10 burpees
- 10 lateral bounds (each

Week 9

Acclimation

Bike cleaning

Important Notes:

- ☐ Two weeks out from our first open-water swim; make sure you've got a wetsuit, an open-water safety buoy, and a calm, low-traffic body of water ready
- ☐ By now your bike is probably sticky with Gatorade, and caked with road grime; give it wash – a dirty chain = a slow bike. Here's how.

M	Tu	W	Th	F	Sa	Su
Rest	S - 1,500 W - KBC	B - 14 mi.	S - 1,500 W - RC	R - 6 mi.	B - 31 mi.	R - 7 mi.

Bike (B)

14 miles
Warmup
• 2 mi @ RPEZ 3-4
Workout
• 2 mi @ RPEZ 3-4
{Repeat 3x}
• 1 mi @ RPEZ 7-8
• 2 mi @ RPEZ 4-5
Cooldown
• 1 mi @ RPEZ 2

31 miles
Warmup
• 2 mi @ RPEZ 2-3
Workout
• 28 mi @ RPEZ 4-5
Cooldown
• 1 mi @ RPEZ 2

Run (R)

6 miles
Warmup
• 0.5 mi @ RPEZ 2-3
Workout
{Repeat 5x}
• 0.25 mi @ RPEZ 8-9
• 0.75 mi @ RPEZ 4-5
Cooldown
• 0.5 mi @ RPEZ 2

7 miles
Warmup
• 0.5 mi @ RPEZ 2-3
Workout
• 6.25 mi @ RPEZ 4-5
Cooldown
• 0.25 mi @ RPEZ 2

Week 10
Acclimation

Training phases

Important Notes:

- Next week we transition into the "Build Phase" of training; it shouldn't feel different week-by-week, but over the course of five weeks we'll be stacking on volume to build your cardiovascular capacity. Curious to learn about training phases? Read this.
- Remind yourself of your Special Something.

M	Tu	W	Th	F	Sa	Su
Rest	S - 1,500 W - BWC	B - 15 mi.	S - 1,500 W - DLC	R - 6 mi.	B - 34 mi.	R - 8 mi.

Bike (B)

15 miles
Warmup
• 2 mi @ RPEZ 3-4
Workout
• 12 mi @ RPEZ 4-5
Cooldown
• 1 mi @ RPEZ 2

34 miles
Warmup
• 2 mi @ RPEZ 2-3
Workout
• 31 mi @ RPEZ 4-5
Cooldown
• 1 mi @ RPEZ 2

Run (R)

6 miles
Warmup
• 0.5 mi @ RPEZ 2-3
Workout
• 5.25 mi @ RPEZ 4-5
Cooldown
• 0.25 mi @ RPEZ 2

8 miles
Warmup
• 0.5 mi @ RPEZ 2-3
Workout
• 7.25 mi @ RPEZ 4-5
Cooldown
• 0.25 mi @ RPEZ 2

Swim (S)

1,500 yds.
Warmup
• 1x100 freestyle
• 1x100 pull
• 1x100 kick

Workout
{15 sec rest between each of 10 sets}
• 8x50 freestyle
• 3x100 pull
• 2x100 kick
• 4x50 freestyle down, choice back

Cooldown
• 1x50 freestyle
• 1x50 choice

1,500 yds.
Warmup
• 1x100 freestyle
• 1x100 pull
• 1x100 kick

Workout
{15 sec rest between each of 14 sets}
• 6x100 freestyle
• 1x100 pull
• 2x50 kick
• 6x50 freestyle down, choice back

Cooldown
• 1x50 freestyle
• 1x50 choice

Weights (W)

Bodyweight Circuit (BWC)
Repeat 3-4x
• 10 squats
• 20 single-leg lunges (10 each)
• 10 push-ups
• 20 mountain climbers
• 10 plank jacks
• Rest 1 min

Dumbbell Leg Circuit (DLC)
Repeat 3-4x
• 10 dumbbell squats
• 10 dumbbell deadlifts
• 10 dumbbell lunges (each leg)
• 10 dumbbell step-ups (each leg)
• 10 calf raises
• Rest for 1 minute

The world is full of people who say "someday I should."
A shining few will apply themselves for long enough
To turn aspirations into action,
And compound action into reality.

The doers.

Up next: The Base Phase. In this phase we'll build
up your baseline endurance, introduce open-water
swimming, and "brick" workouts.

Week 11

Base Phase

Open-water swimming

Important Notes:

☐ This week you'll do your first open-water swim; if you aren't able for whatever reason, skip it rather than doing a third swim workout. This workout is intended to prepare you mentally for open water. Target 1,000 yards of freestyle volume, and <u>read this</u> beforehand.

M	Tu	W	Th	F	Sa	Su
Rest	S - 1,600 W - PC	B - 16 mi.	S - 1,700 W - SBC	R - 4 mi.	B - 37 mi.	S - OW R - 8 mi.

Bike (B)

16 miles
Warmup
• 2 mi @ RPEZ 3-4
Workout
• 13 mi @ RPEZ 4-5
Cooldown
• 1 mi @ RPEZ 2

37 miles
Warmup
• 2 mi @ RPEZ 2-3
Workout
• 34 mi @ RPEZ 4-5
Cooldown
• 1 mi @ RPEZ 2

Run (R)

4 miles
Warmup
• 0.5 mi @ RPEZ 2-3
Workout
• 3.25 mi @ RPEZ 5-6
Cooldown
• 0.25 mi @ RPEZ 2

8 miles
Warmup
• 0.5 mi @ RPEZ 2-3
Workout
• 7.25 mi @ RPEZ 4-5
Cooldown
• 0.25 mi @ RPEZ 2

Swim (S)

1,600 yds.
Warmup
• 2x100 freestyle
• 1x100 pull
• 2x50 kick

Workout

1,700 yds.
Warmup
• 2x100 freestyle
• 1x100 pull
• 2x50 kick

Workout

Weights (W)

Plyometric Circuit (PC)
Repeat 4x
• 10 box jumps
• 10 jump squats
• 10 jump lunges (each leg)
• 10 burpees
• 10 lateral bounds (each

Week 12
Base Phase

Brick workouts

Important Notes:

☐ This week we'll introduce a new workout type: a "brick." To brick is to do two workouts consecutively with a pit-stop-like transition between them. Don't worry about how fast you transition; we're just working on getting your body used to switching modes from biking to running. We'll work on transitions in week 21. Read about brick workouts here.

M	Tu	W	Th	F	Sa	Su
Rest	S - 1,700 W - KBC	B - 15 mi.	S - 1,700 W - RC	R - 6 mi.	B - 33 mi. R - 1 mi.	R - 8 mi.

Bike (B)

15 miles
Warmup
• 2 mi @ RPEZ 3-4
Workout
• 3 mi @ RPEZ 3-4
{Repeat below 3x}
• 1 mi @ RPEZ 7-8
• 2 mi @ RPEZ 4-5
Cooldown
• 1 mi @ RPEZ 2

33 mile "brick"
Warmup
• 2 mi @ RPEZ 2-3
Workout
• 30 mi @ RPEZ 4-5

Transition to run
• 1 mi @ RPEZ 3-4

Run (R)

6 miles
Warmup
• 0.5 mi @ RPEZ 2-3
Workout
• 1.25 mi @ RPEZ 4-5

{Repeat 4x}
• 0.25 mi @ RPEZ 8-9
• 0.75 mi @ RPEZ 4-5
Cooldown

8 miles
Warmup
• 0.5 mi @ RPEZ 2-3
Workout
• 7.75 mi @ RPEZ 4-5
Cooldown
• 0.25 mi @ RPEZ 2

Week 13

Base Phase

Important Notes:

- Swim volume is really ramping; if you're struggling to get this volume done within the pool time you have (average pace slower than 2:30/100yds), you'd probably get a lot of value from talking to your Masters coach, and asking for a few drill recommendations.
- Second open-water swim; shoot for 1,000yds. of total freestyle swimming

M	Tu	W	Th	F	Sa	Su
Rest	S - 1,800 W - BWC	B - 18 mi.	S - 1,900 W - DLC	R - 6 mi.	B - 40 mi.	S - OW R - 9 mi.

Bike (B)

18 miles
Warmup
• 2 mi @ RPEZ 3-4
Workout
• 15 mi @ RPEZ 4-5
Cooldown
• 1 mi @ RPEZ 2

40 miles
Warmup
• 2 mi @ RPEZ 2-3
Workout
• 37 mi @ RPEZ 4-5
Cooldown
• 1 mi @ RPEZ 2

Run (R)

6 miles
Warmup
• 0.5 mi @ RPEZ 2-3
Workout
• 5.25 mi @ RPEZ 4-5
Cooldown
• 0.25 mi @ RPEZ 2

9 miles
Warmup
• 0.5 mi @ RPEZ 2-3
Workout
• 8.25 mi @ RPEZ 4-5
Cooldown
• 0.25 mi @ RPEZ 2

Week 14
Base Phase

Important Notes:

☐ At this point in training "fueling," the concept of eating to replace lost water and nutrients, becomes an important aspect of successfully completing your workouts. Fueling is also often referred to as the "fourth discipline of Ironman." Check the nutrition section on the following pages.

M	Tu	W	Th	F	Sa	Su
Rest	S - 2,000 W - PC	B - 19 mi.	S - 2,100 W - SBC	R - 5 mi.	B - 43 mi. R - 1.5 mi.	R - 9 mi.

Bike (B)

19 miles
Warmup
• 2 mi @ RPEZ 3-4
Workout
• 16 mi @ RPEZ 4-5
Cooldown
• 1 mi @ RPEZ 2

43 mile "brick"
Warmup
• 2 mi @ RPEZ 2-3
Workout
• 41 mi @ RPEZ 4-5

Transition to run
• 1.5 mi @ RPEZ 3-4

Run (R)

5 miles
Warmup
• 0.5 mi @ RPEZ 2-3
Workout
• 4.25 mi @ RPEZ 5-6
Cooldown
• 0.25 mi @ RPEZ 2

9 miles
Warmup
• 0.5 mi @ RPEZ 2-3
Workout
• 8.25 mi @ RPEZ 4-5
Cooldown
• 0.25 mi @ RPEZ 2

Swim (S)

2,000 yds.
Warmup
• 2x100 freestyle
• 1x100 pull
• 2x50 kick

Workout
{15 sec rest between each of 10 sets}
• 2x200 freestyle
• 6x100 freestyle
• 2x100 pull
• 6x50 freestyle sprint

Cooldown
• 1x50 freestyle
• 1x50 choice

2,100 yds.
Warmup
• 2x100 freestyle
• 1x100 pull
• 2x50 kick

Workout
{15 sec rest between each of 12 sets}
• 2x300 freestyle
• 5x100 freestyle
• 2x100 pull
• 6x50 freestyle sprint

Cooldown
• 1x50 freestyle
• 1x50 choice

Weights (W)

Plyometric Circuit (PC)
Repeat 4x
• 10 box jumps
• 10 jump squats
• 10 jump lunges (each leg)
• 10 burpees
• 10 lateral bounds (each direction)
• Rest for 1 minute

Stability Ball Circuit (SBC)
Repeat 4x
• 10 dumbbell squats
• 10 dumbbell deadlifts
• 10 dumbbell lunges (each leg)
• 10 dumbbell step-ups (each leg)
• 10 calf raises
• Rest for 1 minute

NUTRITION

RITION

ten said that "nutrition is the fourth discipline of Ironman;" all the training ʻillpower in the world won't be enough to overcome a bad nutrition plan, so take this section to heart, and practice nutrition with the same dedication you have for the other disciplines.

There are three, broad categories of nutrition for triathlon:
1. "Fueling" - what you consume while racing or working out
2. "Carb loading" - What you consume before a competition
3. General nutrition - What you consume day-to-day during training.

In this section, we're going to focus on numbers one and two: "fueling" and "carb loading."

Fueling

The purpose of fueling is simply to replace the nutrients you lose during competition. Those nutrients are primarily:
- Carbohydrates - these get broken down into energy, and consumed by your body
- Electrolytes - are used by your muscles when they contract
- Water - gets sweated out

To build a fueling plan, you've gotta first figure out how much of these nutrients you're losing as you swim, bike and run. You'll do that by conducting "sweat studies."

Sweat Study

Sweat studies are designed to measure how much water and electrolytes an athlete loses while exercising. The process is simple – just weigh yourself (and your fuel) before and after the workout.

Here's how: before your workout, weigh yourself (without clothes), then weigh all of the water + food you plan to eat/drink. You'll get numbers like this:

> Bodyweight = 150lbs.
> Fuel weight = 60 oz. (3.75lbs.)

After you weigh, go do your workout, as planned. When you return, weigh yourself and your fuel again to figure out how much water you lost in sweat.

Sweat Study (continued)

Following the same example: when you weigh yourself after your workout you get these numbers like these:

> *Bodyweight = 148lbs.*
> *Fuel weight = 12oz (0.75lbs)*

You actually consumed only 48oz. of the 60oz you brought (60 - 12 = 48), so the net addition was 48oz, or 3lbs.

You've got all the data you need, now put it all together to find "x," the amount of weight you lost to sweat:

> *(Before) Bodyweight = 150lbs.*
> *- Sweat   = x*
> *+ Fuel   = 3lbs.*
> _____
> *= (After) Bodyweight = 148lbs.*
>
> *So "x," Sweat Loss = 5lbs.*

Divide that by the amount of time you spent working out (in hours) – let's say here this was two hours:

> *80oz./2hrs. = **40oz./hr.***

You lost 40oz. per hour during your workout. This is your "sweat rate."

You need to repeat this same process at least five times for both the bike and the run.

Log your sweat rates in a notebook, so you can hone in on an average sweat rate for the two longest, sweatiest disciplines: bike and run.

Hydration Plan

With your sweat study journal entries logged, you'll start to establish a trend; let's imagine these are yours:

- Running - 40oz./hr.
- Biking   - 30oz./hr.

Using those figures, you now have what you need to build a hydration plan:

If you're preparing to bike for four hours, you'll need 30oz. x 4 = 120oz.

Great; that's it, right? Not quite...

These are big numbers that you've gotta hit, on average over the course of a race or workout, but to make it actionable, and avoid panic-chugging to catch up, it's helpful to break those averages down into an action plan made of things that you can complete in an easy, repeatable checklist. Here's how that might look:

Every 10 minutes:

- Drink 5oz. of water

Set your smart watch to alert you every 10 minutes, and you're set. There...now you've got a hydration plan that you can execute.

Hydration Logistics

Now that you know how to calculate your way to a hydration plan, you might be a step ahead and already wondering "how do I fit 120oz. of water on my bike?"

It's less of a problem come race day, where you'll have fuel stations every 20 miles or so, but during training it's a real logistical challenge – especially if you're a heavy sweater.

You bike should come stock two water bottle cages; each bottle should fit about 30oz. of water.

If you need more, and you probably will, you can add two more cages and bottles behind your seat, bringing your capacity to 120oz.

Still need more? You can add a fifth bottle to your aero bars, bringing you to 150oz.

SWEAT STUDIES

You can use the following pages as a workbook to log your sweat studies. The example below uses the same numbers to illustrate the previous pages; reference those to see how to get these measurements.

	Lbs.		
1 Fuel (pre-workout)	3.75	**2** Bodyweight (pre-workout, lbs)	150
3 - Fuel (post-workout)	0.75	+ Fuel consumption (lbs)	3.00
4 = Fuel consumption	3.00	**5** - Bodyweight (post-workout, lbs)	148
		6 = Sweat loss (lbs.)	5.00
	Hours	**7** x 16 = Sweat loss (ounces)	80
8 Workout duration	2	**9** / duration = Sweat rate (oz./hr.)	40

1 Put all your fuel on a food scale and weigh it.

2 Then, get on a bathroom scale and weigh your body, and go do your workout.

3 After you finish the workout, weigh your fuel again, and

4 Subtract ③ from ① to find your fuel consumption; plug that number in the table to the right

5 Go shower, dry off, and get on the scale to weigh your body post-workout.

6 Add your consumed fuel ④ to your pre-workout body weight ②, and subtract your post-workout bodyweight ⑤ to find your total sweat loss weight in pounds

7 Multiply your sweat loss weight from ⑥ by 16 to convert that weight to ounces.

8 How long was your workout (in hours)? If it was 1 hour and 15 minutes, that's 1.25, for example. Put that number here.

9 Finally divide your sweat loss in ounces, ⑦, by the duration of your workout in hours, ⑧ to arrive at your sweat rate per hour.

Bike or Run? _____

How did you fuel? _____
_____
_____

Lbs.

Fuel (pre-workout) ☐

- Fuel (post-workout) ☐

= Fuel consumption ☐

Hours

Workout duration ☐

Bodyweight (pre-workout, lbs) ☐

+ Fuel consumption (lbs) ☐

- Bodyweight (post-workout, lbs) ☐

= Sweat loss (lbs.) ☐

x 16 = Sweat loss (ounces) ☐

/ duration = Sweat rate (oz./hr.) ☐

How did it feel? _____
_____
_____

Bike or Run? _____

How did you fuel? _____
_____
_____

Lbs.

Fuel (pre-workout) ☐

- Fuel (post-workout) ☐

= Fuel consumption ☐

Hours

Workout duration ☐

Bodyweight (pre-workout, lbs) ☐

+ Fuel consumption (lbs) ☐

- Bodyweight (post-workout, lbs) ☐

= Sweat loss (lbs.) ☐

x 16 = Sweat loss (ounces) ☐

/ duration = Sweat rate (oz./hr.) ☐

How did it feel? _____
_____
_____

Bike or Run? _____

How did you fuel? _____
_____
_____

	Lbs.		
Fuel (pre-workout)		Bodyweight (pre-workout, lbs)	
- Fuel (post-workout)		+ Fuel consumption (lbs)	
= Fuel consumption		- Bodyweight (post-workout, lbs)	
		= Sweat loss (lbs.)	
	Hours		
Workout duration		x 16 = Sweat loss (ounces)	
		/ duration = Sweat rate (oz./hr.)	

How did it feel? _____
_____
_____

Bike or Run? _____

How did you fuel? _____
_____
_____

	Lbs.		
Fuel (pre-workout)		Bodyweight (pre-workout, lbs)	
- Fuel (post-workout)		+ Fuel consumption (lbs)	
= Fuel consumption		- Bodyweight (post-workout, lbs)	
		= Sweat loss (lbs.)	
	Hours		
Workout duration		x 16 = Sweat loss (ounces)	
		/ duration = Sweat rate (oz./hr.)	

How did it feel? _____
_____
_____

Bike or Run? _____

How did you fuel? _____
_____
_____

	Lbs.
Fuel (pre-workout)	
- Fuel (post-workout)	
= Fuel consumption	

	Hours
Workout duration	

Bodyweight (pre-workout, lbs)	
+ Fuel consumption (lbs)	
- Bodyweight (post-workout, lbs)	
= Sweat loss (lbs.)	
x 16 = Sweat loss (ounces)	
/ duration = Sweat rate (oz./hr.)	

How did it feel? _____
_____
_____

Bike or Run? _____

How did you fuel? _____
_____
_____

	Lbs.
Fuel (pre-workout)	
- Fuel (post-workout)	
= Fuel consumption	

	Hours
Workout duration	

Bodyweight (pre-workout, lbs)	
+ Fuel consumption (lbs)	
- Bodyweight (post-workout, lbs)	
= Sweat loss (lbs.)	
x 16 = Sweat loss (ounces)	
/ duration = Sweat rate (oz./hr.)	

How did it feel? _____
_____
_____

Bike or Run? _____

How did you fuel? _____
_____
_____

	Lbs.		

Fuel (pre-workout)

- Fuel (post-workout)

= Fuel consumption

Hours

Workout duration

Bodyweight (pre-workout, lbs)

+ Fuel consumption (lbs)

- Bodyweight (post-workout, lbs)

= Sweat loss (lbs.)

x 16 = Sweat loss (ounces)

/ duration = Sweat rate (oz./hr.)

How did it feel? _____
_____
_____

Bike or Run? _____

How did you fuel? _____
_____
_____

Lbs.

Fuel (pre-workout)

- Fuel (post-workout)

= Fuel consumption

Hours

Workout duration

Bodyweight (pre-workout, lbs)

+ Fuel consumption (lbs)

- Bodyweight (post-workout, lbs)

= Sweat loss (lbs.)

x 16 = Sweat loss (ounces)

/ duration = Sweat rate (oz./hr.)

How did it feel? _____
_____
_____

Bike or Run? _____

How did you fuel? _____
_____
_____

Lbs.

Fuel (pre-workout) [ ] Bodyweight (pre-workout, lbs) [ ]

- Fuel (post-workout) [ ] + Fuel consumption (lbs) [ ]

= Fuel consumption [ ] - Bodyweight (post-workout, lbs) [ ]

= Sweat loss (lbs.) [ ]

Hours

Workout duration [ ] x 16 = Sweat loss (ounces) [ ]

/ duration = Sweat rate (oz./hr.) [ ]

How did it feel? _____
_____
_____

Bike or Run? _____

How did you fuel? _____
_____
_____

Lbs.

Fuel (pre-workout) [ ] Bodyweight (pre-workout, lbs) [ ]

- Fuel (post-workout) [ ] + Fuel consumption (lbs) [ ]

= Fuel consumption [ ] - Bodyweight (post-workout, lbs) [ ]

= Sweat loss (lbs.) [ ]

Hours

Workout duration [ ] x 16 = Sweat loss (ounces) [ ]

/ duration = Sweat rate (oz./hr.) [ ]

How did it feel? _____
_____
_____

Carbohydrate Plan

There are two different types of carbohydrates ("carbs"):
1. Complex
2. Simple

Complex carbs are broken down more slowly by your body, and take longer to deliver energy. Simple carbs – the kind you need while training or racing – are easy for the body to break down, so they can rapidly be transformed into the energy you need.

All of these carb sources are commonly eaten by other triathletes:

- Bananas
- Raisins
- Honey
- Crackers
- Pretzels
- Candy bars
- Sports drinks
- Dates
- BP&J sandwiches
- Gu packets
- Gummy candy
- Marshmallows

There's no scientific method for figuring out your carb intake, nor – more importantly: to figure out which foods work best with your body. The best method is to simply start by targeting 60g of carbs per hour, and adjust from there.

If you're having "gastrointestinal distress" shall we say, dial back on the carbs or try a different source of carbs.

If you're feeling sluggish, sleepy, or just over tired, you should up your carbs or – again – try another source of carbs.

If you plan to drink a fluid that also has carbs (and electrolytes), you need to take those nutrients into account when making your plan.

So, again, let's walk through it by extending the previous example: you're getting ready for a 4 hour bike ride, you'll bring 120oz. of fluid, as we've already established (on the previous pages).

All 120oz. will be Gatorade, which has 1.8g of carbs per ounce.

So we've got 216g of carbs "on board" in the Gatorade we've got bottled and ready:

$$1.8g \times 120oz. = 216g$$

But we want to consume 60g/hr for four hours – that's 240g (60g x 4hr), so we need to add another 30g of carbs throughout the workout.

So we add one Smucker's Uncrustable, which has 36g of carbs, into our jersey, and plan to eat about 1/3rd at hours 1, 2, and 3.

Now, our plan looks like this:

> *Every 10 minutes*
> - *Drink 5oz. Gatorade*
>
> *Every Hour*
> - *Eat one bite of Uncrustable*

Electrolyte Plan

In the same way we've treated carbs and water previously, you'd also treat electrolytes – in this case primarily salt.

The best method for figuring out how much salt you lose in sweat is to use Gatorade Sweat Patches, and the accompanying smartphone app.

Those patches will help you find your salt loss rate, but let's imagine, for sake of example, that you lose 1,000mg of salt per hour on the bike.

We know we've already got 120oz. of Gatorade – fluid plan: done. We know we need another 30g of Carbs. Carbs: done. But what about electrolytes?

You've already found that you lose 1,000mg of salt per hour.

The Uncrustable is going to give us back 220mg, and the Gatorade we're planning to drink is going to give us back another 1,620mg:

Gatorade: 120oz. x 13.5 = 1,620mg
Uncrustable: 1 x 220mg = 220mg
TOTAL = 1,840mg

But that's well short of what we're going to lose in sweat 4,000mg:

$$1,000mg/hr \times 4hr = 4,000mg$$

So we've gotta add 2,160mg (4,000 - 1,840) of salt to our fuel plan, so we mix in ¼ teaspoon of table salt into each of our four water bottles, and plan to drink them as previously planned.

The Finished Plan

By taking the time to measure our rate of loss for carbs, electrolytes, and water, we've been able to come up with a simple, easy-to-follow nutrition plan that keep you performing at your peak, and focused on the race – not your fueling.

> *Every 10 minutes*
> - *Drink 5oz. Salty Gatorade*
>
> *Every Hour*
> - *Eat one bite of Uncrustable*

"Carb Loading"

When carbohydrates are consumed, they are broken down into glucose and stored in the muscles and liver as glycogen.

The body can store a limited amount of glycogen, and once those stores are depleted, performance declines.

However, by consuming a high-carbohydrate diet and tapering exercise leading up to an event, the body can increase its glycogen stores beyond the normal limit, improving endurance performance and delaying fatigue.

Leading up to race day, you'll have weekend workouts that grow progressively longer, eventually hitting 18mi. on the run, and 100mi. on the bike.

These are workouts that you can – and should "carb load" for. It'll help you perform better, but – more importantly – it'll give you a chance to figure out what meals work best for your body.

Too many athletes think it's pasta alone that they should be eating; pasta is a great "carb load" meal, but there are many other great options. Here are some ideal types of food for carb loading:

Ideal Carb Loading Foods

Complex carbohydrates: whole grains, brown rice, quinoa, and sweet potatoes.

Fruits and vegetables: Fruits and vegetables are rich in vitamins, minerals, and fiber, and also provide a source of carbohydrates.

High-carbohydrate snacks: Snacks such as energy bars, gels, and fruit juice can also be used to top off glycogen in the moments just before an event.

Low-fat proteins: Lean proteins such as chicken, fish, and tofu can be incorporated into meals to provide amino acids for muscle repair without adding excess fat or calories that can compromise carbohydrate intake.

Week 15

Base Phase

Important Notes:

- ☐ Open-water swim: shoot for 1,200yds. of volume, and try to get one sustained, longer leg of 400 yards or more
- ☐ Don't be afraid to mix in a yoga workout in lieu for one of your strength training sessions each week. You'll still get plenty of strength training, and you'll get some much-needed stretching.

M	Tu	W	Th	F	Sa	Su
Rest	S - 1,700 W - KBC	B - 19 mi.	S - 1,700 W - RC	S - OW R - 3 mi.	B - 46 mi. R - 2 mi.	R - 10 mi.

Bike (B)

19 miles
Warmup
• 2 mi @ RPEZ 3-4
Workout
• 7 mi @ RPEZ 3-4
{Repeat 3x}
• 1 mi @ RPEZ 7-8
• 2 mi @ RPEZ 4-5
Cooldown
• 1 mi @ RPEZ 2

46 mile "brick"
Warmup
• 2 mi @ RPEZ 2-3
Workout
• 44 mi @ RPEZ 4-5

Transition to run
• 2 mi @ RPEZ 3-4

Run (R)

3 miles
Warmup
• 0.5 mi @ RPEZ 2-3
Workout
• 2.25 mi @ RPEZ 4-5
Cooldown
• 0.25 mi @ RPEZ 2

10 miles
Warmup
• 0.5 mi @ RPEZ 2-3
Workout
• 9.25 mi @ RPEZ 4-5
Cooldown
• 0.25 mi @ RPEZ 2

Week 16

Base Phase

Important Notes:

- [ ] We're doing a lot of work now to add on bike volume. To balance training, running is staying pretty steady. Don't worry; you're right on track.
- [ ] Pro tip: put a plastic grocery bag over your foot before pulling on your wetsuit; it'll help your foot glide past your suit with ease

M	Tu	W	Th	F	Sa	Su
Rest	S - 2,100 W - BWC	B - 18 mi.	S - 2,100 W - DLC	R - 6 mi.	B - 41 mi. R - 2.5 mi.	R - 9 mi.

Bike (B)

18 miles
Warmup
• 2 mi @ RPEZ 3-4
Workout
• 15 mi @ RPEZ 4-5
Cooldown
• 1 mi @ RPEZ 2

41 mile "brick"
Warmup
• 2 mi @ RPEZ 2-3
Workout
• 39 mi @ RPEZ 4-5

Transition to run
• 2.5 mi @ RPEZ 3-4

Run (R)

6 miles
Warmup
• 0.5 mi @ RPEZ 2-3
Workout
• 5.25 mi @ RPEZ 4-5
Cooldown
• 0.25 mi @ RPEZ 2

9 miles
Warmup
• 0.5 mi @ RPEZ 2-3
Workout
• 8.25 mi @ RPEZ 4-5
Cooldown
• 0.25 mi @ RPEZ 2

Week 17

Base Phase

Important Notes:

☐ Trying to figure out how to hydrate during long runs? Try this: set out water bottles in your driveway, and find a route that you can loop several times, taking you past your house. Grab your drink as you pass by each time.

M	Tu	W	Th	F	Sa	Su
Rest	S - 2,100 W - PC	B - 21 mi.	S - 2,100 W - SBC	R - 5 mi.	B - 49 mi. R - 2 mi.	R - 11 mi.

Bike (B)

21 miles
Warmup
• 2 mi @ RPEZ 3-4
Workout
• 18 mi @ RPEZ 4-5
Cooldown
• 1 mi @ RPEZ 2

49 miles
Warmup
• 2 mi @ RPEZ 2-3
Workout
• 47 mi @ RPEZ 4-5

Transition to run
• 2 mi @ RPEZ 3-4

Run (R)

5 miles
Warmup
• 0.5 mi @ RPEZ 2-3
Workout
• 4.75 mi @ RPEZ 5-6
Cooldown
• 0.25 mi @ RPEZ 2

11 miles
Warmup
• 0.5 mi @ RPEZ 2-3
Workout
• 10.75 mi @ RPEZ 4-5
Cooldown
• 0.25 mi @ RPEZ 2

Week 18

Base Phase

Important Notes:

- ☐ Open-water swim: these sessions have little to do with training volume, and everything to do with building psychological readiness for race day. Find ways to challenge your mental barriers while staying safe.
- ☐ Pro tip: you can store your valuables in your swim buoy while you swim – it's waterproof

M	Tu	W	Th	F	Sa	Su
Rest	S - 2,100 W - KBC	B - 22 mi.	S - 2,100 W - RC	S - OW R - 5 mi.	B - 52 mi. R - 3.5 mi.	R - 11 mi.

Bike (B)

22 miles
Warmup
• 2 mi @ RPEZ 3-4
Workout
• 8 mi @ RPEZ 3-4
{Repeat 4x}
• 1 mi @ RPEZ 7-8
• 2 mi @ RPEZ 4-5
Cooldown
• 1 mi @ RPEZ 2

52 mile "brick"
Warmup
• 2 mi @ RPEZ 2-3
Workout
• 50 mi @ RPEZ 4-5

Transition to run
• 3.5 mi @ RPEZ 3-4

Run (R)

5 miles
Warmup
• 0.5 mi @ RPEZ 2-3
Workout
• 1.25 mi @ RPEZ 4-5

{Repeat 3x}
• 0.25 mi @ RPEZ 8-9
• 0.75 mi @ RPEZ 4-5
Cooldown

11 miles
Warmup
• 0.5 mi @ RPEZ 2-3
Workout
• 10.25 mi @ RPEZ 4-5
Cooldown
• 0.25 mi @ RPEZ 2

Base Phase

Important Notes:

- ☐ It's never fun to train in the rain, but it can be handy – never know what kind of conditions you'll encounter on race day.
- ☐ Experiment with different types of fuel to figure out what works best for your body; you'll want to have this dialed in well before race day.

M	Tu	W	Th	F	Sa	Su
Rest	S - 2,100 W - BWC	B - 23 mi.	S - 2,100 W - DLC	R - 4 mi.	B - 55 mi. R - 2 mi.	R - 11 mi.

Bike (B)

23 miles
Warmup
- 2 mi @ RPEZ 3-4
Workout
- 20 mi @ RPEZ 4-5
Cooldown
- 1 mi @ RPEZ 2

55 miles
Warmup
- 2 mi @ RPEZ 2-3
Workout
- 53 mi @ RPEZ 4-5

Transition to run
- 2 mi @ RPEZ 3-4

Run (R)

4 miles
Warmup
- 0.5 mi @ RPEZ 2-3
Workout
- 3.25 mi @ RPEZ 4-5
Cooldown
- 0.25 mi @ RPEZ 2

11 miles
Warmup
- 0.5 mi @ RPEZ 2-3
Workout
- 10.25 mi @ RPEZ 4-5
Cooldown
- 0.25 mi @ RPEZ 2

Swim (S)

2,100 yds.
Warmup
- 2x100 freestyle
- 1x100 pull
- 1x100 kick

Workout
{15 sec rest between each of 10 sets}
- 2x400 freestyle
- 4x100 freestyle
- 2x100 pull
- 4x50 freestyle down, choice back

Cooldown
- 1x50 freestyle
- 1x50 choice

2,100 yds.
Warmup
- 1x100 freestyle
- 2x100 pull
- 1x100 kick

Workout
{15 sec rest between each of 14 sets}
- 2x400 freestyle
- 4x100 freestyle
- 2x100 pull
- 4x50 freestyle down, choice back

Cooldown
- 1x50 freestyle
- 1x50 choice

Weights (W)

Bodyweight Circuit (BWC)
Repeat 3-4x
- 10 squats
- 20 single-leg lunges (10 each)
- 10 push-ups
- 20 mountain climbers
- 10 plank jacks
- Rest 1 min

Dumbbell Leg Circuit (DLC)
Repeat 3-4x
- 10 dumbbell squats
- 10 dumbbell deadlifts
- 10 dumbbell lunges (each leg)
- 10 dumbbell step-ups (each leg)
- 10 calf raises
- Rest for 1 minute

Week 20

Base Phase

Important Notes:

- ☐ Trying to figure out how to hydrate during long runs? Try this: set out water bottles in your driveway, and find a route that you can loop several times, taking you past your house. Grab your drink as you pass by.

M	Tu	W	Th	F	Sa	Su
Rest	S - 2,100 W - PC	B - 20 mi.	S - 2,100 W - SBC	R - 7 mi.	B - 50 mi. R - 2 mi.	R - 11 mi.

Bike (B)

20 miles
Warmup
- 2 mi @ RPEZ 3-4
Workout
- 17 mi @ RPEZ 4-5
Cooldown
- 1 mi @ RPEZ 2

50 miles
Warmup
- 2 mi @ RPEZ 2-3
Workout
- 48 mi @ RPEZ 4-5

Transition to run
- 2 mi @ RPEZ 3-4

Run (R)

7 miles
Warmup
- 0.5 mi @ RPEZ 2-3
Workout
- 6.25 mi @ RPEZ 5-6
Cooldown
- 0.25 mi @ RPEZ 2

11 miles
Warmup
- 0.5 mi @ RPEZ 2-3
Workout
- 10.25 mi @ RPEZ 4-5
Cooldown
- 0.25 mi @ RPEZ 2

Swim (S)

2,100 yds.
Warmup
- 2x100 freestyle
- 1x100 pull
- 2x50 kick

Workout
{15 sec rest between each of 10 sets}
- 3x200 freestyle
- 5x100 freestyle
- 2x100 pull
- 6x50 freestyle sprint

Cooldown
- 1x50 freestyle
- 1x50 choice

2,100 yds.
Warmup
- 1x100 freestyle
- 2x100 pull
- 2x50 kick

Workout
{15 sec rest between each of 12 sets}
- 2x300 freestyle
- 4x100 freestyle
- 3x100 pull
- 6x50 freestyle sprint

Cooldown
- 1x50 freestyle
- 1x50 choice

Weights (W)

Plyometric Circuit (PC)
Repeat 4x
- 10 box jumps
- 10 jump squats
- 10 jump lunges (each leg)
- 10 burpees
- 10 lateral bounds (each direction)
- Rest for 1 minute

Stability Ball Circuit (SBC)
Repeat 4x
- 10 dumbbell squats
- 10 dumbbell deadlifts
- 10 dumbbell lunges (each leg)
- 10 dumbbell step-ups (each leg)
- 10 calf raises
- Rest for 1 minute

"You are braver than you believe,
stronger than you seem, and
smarter than you think."

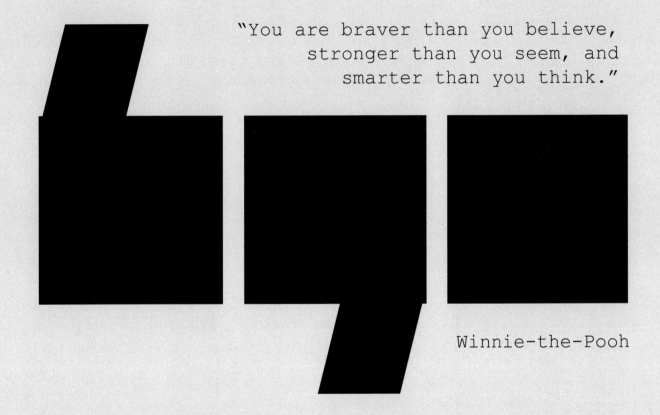

Winnie-the-Pooh

TRANSITIONS

The reality is, unless you're gunning for a place on the podium, your transitions are less about speed, and more about efficiency.

The folks standing on the podium are looking to save seconds; we're going to tell you how to save *minutes* by planning, preparing, and practicing for smooth and efficient transitions.

The "Tri Suit"

A tri suit is a one-piece garment that is made of a stretchy and lightweight material that is quick-drying, breathable, and designed to be worn for all three legs of the race - the swim, bike, and run.

95% of athletes in an Ironman will opt to wear one of these because it's incredibly easy and efficient. With a tri suit, you don't need to find a private change area in the first transition ("T1"), and can simply strip down to your tri suit at your bike station before going out on the bike.

We didn't include this in the quick-start gear checklist because it's not *required.* You could get by without it, and some people do, but it's sure nice to have, and will – certainly – shave minutes off your finish time.

"T1" Swim-to-Bike Transition

A good swim transition starts before you ever get into the water. By preparing your wetsuit and swim-to-bike transition gear is ready, you can save wasted effort, and time.

It starts with your wetsuit. When you suit up, make sure the tag end of the rope attached to your zipper is secured under the flap of your wetsuit. This will help you be able to easily grab and unzip when you exit the water.

Coming out of the water you'll be wet (obvi.), a little dizzy (probably), and tired (almost certainly). It's way too common that athletes will try to run out of the water, slip, and fall – usually on a concrete boat ramp.

Don't do that.

Here's a better plan: walk – slowly – out of the water. Once you're on dry land, you should focus on getting yourself ready for the transition. Pull off your swim cap, goggles, and top half of your wetsuit, leaving your legs covered by the wetsuit for now.

If you feel like jogging at this point, go for it.

Savvy triathletes take time the day prior to the race to walk the T1 transition, from water's edge all the way to their bike, noting big, visual landmarks they can reference to quickly find the way to their bike the next day.

When you get to your bike, you'll want to have a two towels alrieady laid out at your station:

The first, a very brightly colored or visually distinct one (so you can quickly spot your bike). You'll fold this and put it on your bike handlebars, and use it to dry your body and face.

The other, you'll put on the ground beside your bike, and stand on it while you change, so you can get the sand and water off your feet (and keep it off).

Once you've got your swim stuff off, and are relatively dry, it's time to dressed and ready for the bike.

Again, a good transition to bike has everything to do with preparation beforehand.

Your bike shoes should be on the towel beside your bike, loosened and ready to put your feet in..

Have your socks ready to go: put them next to your bike shoes, and sprinkle a little baby powder in the sock before the race start – this will help your foot slide in easily even if it's a little wet still.

Again, a good transition to bike is about preparation beforehand.

Your bike shoes should be on the towel beside your bike, loose and ready to go.

Have your socks ready to go: put them next to your bike shoes, and sprinkle a little baby powder in the sock before the race start – this will help your foot slide in easily even if it's a little wet still.

Everything else you'll need on the bike should be *attached to it*.

Hang your helmet off your handlebars. Tape your glasses to your handlebars, and have all your fuel in either your water bottles, a "bento box," or taped to your bike frame (using electrical tape – as shown here).

With your station well prepared beforehand, now you're all set. Everything you need is in its place, ready to go for you.

Get to your station, remove your wetsuit from your legs (use the bike rack for support if you need it), dry off, put on your socks, shoes, and helmet, and then walk your bike to the transition exit (athletes are not allowed to ride their bike until they reach the "mount line").

Walk past the mount line (usually marked with a large, inflatable arch – but always marked with a spray painted line), and get on your bike, like you always do. Don't bust out the "flying mount" for the first time on race day, or you will – almost certainly fall flat on your face.

Once you're on your bike, clipped in, and rolling, now you can detach your sunglasses, and any other gear that you had attached to your bike.

The Ironman is a Little Different

At Ironman-branded races, you will not be allowed to place things like your bike shoes, and socks beneath your race station. You'll store those in a plastic transition bag that will be stored at the entrance of the transition area.

Coming into each transition, you'll find your bag, and carry it to your station. There, you can have whatever accessories you like already attached to your bike.

For now, don't worry about the race bag situation. We'll talk about it in great detail, and help you feel comfortable with every aspect of race-day readiness on page 82.

"T2" Transition to The Run

If T1 is 90% transition efficiency, 10% bodily readiness, T2 is 10% transition efficiency, and 90% bodily readiness – which is why, you'll notice we have lots of T2 "brick" workouts, and zero T1 "bricks."

After biking for roughly five hours your body will be "less than willing" shall we say? So don't neglect the importance of your bricks during training.

Your first few brick workouts will be really slow – that's perfectly normal. Your body needs training to be able to transition from a long bike into a run smoothly.

If we can be honest, it's never going to feel great, but it does get better, and you will get faster – but only if you work at it.

Alright, now for the operational setup for T2: in a non-Ironman event, you'll return to your bike station to rack your bike, and change into your run gear.

At your station, you'll have your:
- running shoes
- socks (if you want to wear a new/different pair for the run)
- race belt (with race number attached)
- running hat
- Backup pair of sunglasses (in case you lose yours during the bike)

Leave your race belt in your shoes, so you can't forget it, and consider adding some baby powder to your new socks – they'll slide on a lot easier.

Once you're ready, you can run – no need to walk through transition, like on the bike.

Week 21
Build Phase

Build Phase: Bike and Run volume will ramp up in this phase, making nutrition an important new variable to consider.

Important Notes:

- ☐ Don't forget to collect sweat studies for both your bike and your run – they'll be different rates; need a refresher? Read about it on page 36.
- ☐ Open-water swims should be feeling a little easier now; if you can, try swimming in a new spot to build your mental resilience; be safe, but take yourself out of your comfort zone.

M	Tu	W	Th	F	Sa	Su
Rest	S - 2,100 W - KBC	B - 25 mi.	S - 2,100 W - RC	S - OW R - 7 mi.	B - 58 mi. R - 2 mi.	R - 12 mi.

Bike (B)

25 miles
Warmup
- 2 mi @ RPEZ 3-4

Workout
{Repeat 5x}
- 1 mi @ RPEZ 7-8
- 2 mi @ RPEZ 4-5

———
- 7 mi @ RPEZ 3-4

Cooldown
- 1 mi @ RPEZ 2

58 mile "brick"
Warmup
- 2 mi @ RPEZ 2-3

Workout
- 56 mi @ RPEZ 4-5

Transition to run
- 2 mi @ RPEZ 3-4

Run (R)

7 miles
Warmup
- 0.5 mi @ RPEZ 2-3

Workout
- 1.25 mi @ RPEZ 4-5

{Repeat 5x}
- 0.25 mi @ RPEZ 8-9
- 0.75 mi @ RPEZ 4-5

Cooldown
- 0.25 mi @ RPEZ 2

12 miles
Warmup
- 0.5 mi @ RPEZ 2-3

Workout
- 11.25 mi @ RPEZ 4-5

Cooldown
- 0.25 mi @ RPEZ 2

Swim (S)

2,100 yds.
Warmup
- 1x100 freestyle
- 4x50 choice
- 4x25 freestyle sprints

Workout
{15 sec rest between each of 12 sets}
- 2x400 freestyle
- 5x100 freestyle
- 4x50 choice
- 4x25 freestyle sprint

Cooldown
- 1x100 freestyle easy
- 1x100 choice

2,100 yds.
Warmup
- 1x100 freestyle
- 2x50 kick
- 2x100 pull

Workout
{20 sec rest between each of 12 sets}
- 2x400 freestyle
- 5x100 freestyle
- 2x100 pull
- 4x25 freestyle sprint

Cooldown
- 1x50 freestyle
- 1x50 choice

Weights (W)

Kettlebell Circuit (KBC)
Repeat 3-4x
- 10 kettlebell swings
- 10 goblet squats
- 10 kettlebell lunges (each leg)
- 20 single-arm kettlebell rows
- Rest for 1 minute

Resistance Circuit (RC)
Repeat 3-4x
- 10 resistance band squats
- 10 resistance band deadlifts
- 20 resistance band lateral walks
- 20 resistance band leg curls
- 10 resistance band glute bridges
- Rest for 1 minute

Week 22
Build Phase

Important Notes:

- You will – at some point – get a flat tire. It's a good idea to carry a spare tube, a CO2 pump, CO2 cartridge, a quick pump, and some tire levers in a saddle bag attached under your seat.
- When you have to run on roads with car traffic, do it on the left shoulder, so you can see oncoming vehicles, and give them plenty of room as they pass.

M	Tu	W	Th	F	Sa	Su
Rest	S - 2,100 W - BWC	B - 26 mi.	S - 2,100 W - DLC	R - 7 mi.	B - 61 mi. R - 2 mi.	R - 13 mi.

Bike (B)

26 miles
Warmup
- 2 mi @ RPEZ 3-4

Workout
- 23 mi @ RPEZ 4-5

Cooldown
- 1 mi @ RPEZ 2

61 miles
Warmup
- 2 mi @ RPEZ 2-3

Workout
- 59 mi @ RPEZ 4-5

Transition to run
- 2 mi @ RPEZ 3-4

Run (R)

7 miles
Warmup
- 0.5 mi @ RPEZ 2-3

Workout
- 6.25 mi @ RPEZ 4-5

Cooldown
- 0.25 mi @ RPEZ 2

13 miles
Warmup
- 0.5 mi @ RPEZ 2-3

Workout
- 12.25 mi @ RPEZ 4-5

Cooldown
- 0.25 mi @ RPEZ 2

Swim (S)

2,100 yds.
Warmup
- 1x100 freestyle
- 1x100 pull
- 1x100 kick

Workout
{15 sec rest between each of 10 sets}
- 2x400 freestyle
- 5x100 freestyle
- 2x100 pull
- 4x50 freestyle down, choice back

Cooldown
- 1x50 freestyle
- 1x50 choice

2,100 yds.
Warmup
- 1x100 freestyle
- 1x100 pull
- 1x100 kick

Workout
{15 sec rest between each of 14 sets}
- 2x400 freestyle
- 4x100 freestyle
- 2x100 pull
- 6x50 freestyle down, choice back

Cooldown
- 1x50 freestyle
- 1x50 choice

Weights (W)

Bodyweight Circuit (BWC)
Repeat 3-4x
- 10 squats
- 20 single-leg lunges (10 each)
- 10 push-ups
- 20 mountain climbers
- 10 plank jacks
- Rest 1 min

Dumbbell Leg Circuit (DLC)
Repeat 3-4x
- 10 dumbbell squats
- 10 dumbbell deadlifts
- 10 dumbbell lunges (each leg)
- 10 dumbbell step-ups (each leg)
- 10 calf raises
- Rest for 1 minute

Build Phase

Important Notes:

☐ Getting blisters on your toes? Check out a pair of toe socks; they'll keep your toes from rubbing together.

☐ Tendon soreness? Freeze water in a paper cup, then peel back the paper so you can use the ice as a massage tool on sore spots – in tandem, cold and massage work wonders.

M	Tu	W	Th	F	Sa	Su
Rest	S - 2,100 W - PC	B - 27 mi.	S - 2,100 W - SBC	R - 5 mi.	B - 64 mi. R - 2 mi.	R - 13 mi.

Bike (B)

27 miles
Warmup
• 2 mi @ RPEZ 3-4
Workout
• 24 mi @ RPEZ 4-5
Cooldown
• 1 mi @ RPEZ 2

64 miles
Warmup
• 2 mi @ RPEZ 2-3
Workout
• 62 mi @ RPEZ 4-5

Transition to run
• 2 mi @ RPEZ 3-4

Run (R)

5 miles
Warmup
• 0.5 mi @ RPEZ 2-3
Workout
• 4.25 mi @ RPEZ 5-6
Cooldown
• 0.25 mi @ RPEZ 2

13 miles
Warmup
• 0.5 mi @ RPEZ 2-3
Workout
• 12.25 mi @ RPEZ 4-5
Cooldown
• 0.25 mi @ RPEZ 2

Swim (S)

2,100 yds.
Warmup
• 2x100 freestyle
• 1x100 pull
• 2x50 kick

Workout
{15 sec rest between each of 10 sets}
• 3x200 freestyle
• 5x100 freestyle
• 2x100 pull
• 6x50 freestyle sprint

Cooldown
• 1x50 freestyle
• 1x50 choice

2,100 yds.
Warmup
• 2x100 freestyle
• 1x100 pull
• 2x50 kick

Workout
{15 sec rest between each of 12 sets}
• 2x300 freestyle
• 4x100 freestyle
• 3x100 pull
• 6x50 freestyle sprint

Cooldown
• 1x50 freestyle
• 1x50 choice

Weights (W)

Plyometric Circuit (PC)
Repeat 4x
• 10 box jumps
• 10 jump squats
• 10 jump lunges (each leg)
• 10 burpees
• 10 lateral bounds (each direction)
• Rest for 1 minute

Stability Ball Circuit (SBC)
Repeat 4x
• 10 dumbbell squats
• 10 dumbbell deadlifts
• 10 dumbbell lunges (each leg)
• 10 dumbbell step-ups (each leg)
• 10 calf raises
• Rest for 1 minute

Week 24

Build Phase

Good running
form

Important Notes:

- ☐ Soreness in the front of your shin is often caused by "heel striking;" if that's you, <u>read this</u>.
- ☐ Put small bandages over your nipples to keep them from chafing on your shirt – it's weird, but someone had to tell you.

M	Tu	W	Th	F	Sa	Su
Rest	S - 2,100 W - KBC	B - 24 mi.	S - 2,100 W - RC	S - OW R - 9 mi.	B - 58 mi. R - 2 mi.	R - 12 mi.

Bike (B)

24 miles
Warmup
• 2 mi @ RPEZ 3-4
Workout
{Repeat 5x}
• 1 mi @ RPEZ 7-8
• 2 mi @ RPEZ 4-5
———
• 6 mi @ RPEZ 3-4
Cooldown
• 1 mi @ RPEZ 2

58 mile "brick"
Warmup
• 2 mi @ RPEZ 2-3
Workout
• 56 mi @ RPEZ 4-5

Transition to run
• 2 mi @ RPEZ 3-4

Run (R)

9 miles
Warmup
• 0.5 mi @ RPEZ 2-3
Workout
• 3.25 mi @ RPEZ 4-5

{Repeat 5x}
• 0.25 mi @ RPEZ 8-9
• 0.75 mi @ RPEZ 4-5
Cooldown
• 0.25 mi @ RPEZ 2

12 miles
Warmup
• 0.5 mi @ RPEZ 2-3
Workout
• 11.25 mi @ RPEZ 4-5
Cooldown
• 0.25 mi @ RPEZ 2

Swim (S)

2,100 yds.
Warmup
• 1x100 freestyle
• 4x50 choice
• 4x25 freestyle sprints

Workout
{15 sec rest between each of 12 sets}
• 2x400 freestyle
• 5x100 freestyle
• 4x50 choice
• 4x25 freestyle sprint

Cooldown

2,100 yds.
Warmup
• 1x100 freestyle
• 2x50 kick
• 2x100 pull

Workout
{20 sec rest between each of 12 sets}
• 2x400 freestyle
• 5x100 freestyle
• 2x100 pull
• 4x25 freestyle sprint

Cooldown

Weights (W)

Kettlebell Circuit (KBC)
Repeat 3-4x
• 10 kettlebell swings
• 10 goblet squats
• 10 kettlebell lunges (each leg)
• 20 single-arm kettlebell rows
• Rest for 1 minute

Resistance Circuit (RC)
Repeat 3-4x
• 10 resistance band squats
• 10 resistance band deadlifts
• 20 resistance band lateral walks
• 20 resistance band leg curls
• 10 resistance band glute bridges

Build Phase

Important Notes:

☐ Take care of your feet. Get high-quality socks, keep 'em dry with talcum powder, and give yourself a pedicure every now and then.

M	Tu	W	Th	F	Sa	Su
Rest	S - 2,100 W - BWC	B - 29 mi.	S - 2,100 W - DLC	R - 8 mi.	B - 67 mi. R - 2 mi.	R - 14 mi.

Bike (B)

29 miles
Warmup
• 2 mi @ RPEZ 3-4
Workout
• 26 mi @ RPEZ 4-5
Cooldown
• 1 mi @ RPEZ 2

67 miles
Warmup
• 2 mi @ RPEZ 2-3
Workout
• 65 mi @ RPEZ 4-5

Transition to run
• 2 mi @ RPEZ 3-4

Run (R)

8 miles
Warmup
• 0.5 mi @ RPEZ 2-3
Workout
• 7.25 mi @ RPEZ 4-5
Cooldown
• 0.25 mi @ RPEZ 2

14 miles
Warmup
• 0.5 mi @ RPEZ 2-3
Workout
• 13.25 mi @ RPEZ 4-5
Cooldown
• 0.25 mi @ RPEZ 2

Swim (S)

2,100 yds.
Warmup
• 1x100 freestyle
• 1x100 pull
• 1x100 kick

Workout
{15 sec rest between each of 10 sets}
• 2x400 freestyle
• 5x100 freestyle
• 2x100 pull
• 4x50 freestyle down, choice back

Cooldown
• 1x50 freestyle
• 1x50 choice

2,100 yds.
Warmup
• 1x100 freestyle
• 1x100 pull
• 1x100 kick

Workout
{15 sec rest between each of 14 sets}
• 2x400 freestyle
• 4x100 freestyle
• 2x100 pull
• 6x50 freestyle down, choice back

Cooldown
• 1x50 freestyle
• 1x50 choice

Weights (W)

Bodyweight Circuit (BWC)
Repeat 3-4x
• 10 squats
• 20 single-leg lunges (10 each)
• 10 push-ups
• 20 mountain climbers
• 10 plank jacks
• Rest 1 min

Dumbbell Leg Circuit (DLC)
Repeat 3-4x
• 10 dumbbell squats
• 10 dumbbell deadlifts
• 10 dumbbell lunges (each leg)
• 10 dumbbell step-ups (each leg)
• 10 calf raises
• Rest for 1 minute

Week 26
Build Phase

Important Notes:

- Fix the minor irritations now: a wetsuit neckline that chafes, a hole in your tri-suit that leads to sunburn, or shoes that give you hotspots on the soles of your feet. While all of these can be minor irritations in training, when it comes to racing an iron-distance triathlon their impact will be magnified.

M	Tu	W	Th	F	Sa	Su
Rest	S - 2,100 W - PC	B - 29 mi.	S - 2,100 W - SBC	R - 6 mi.	B - 70 mi. R - 4 mi.	R - 14 mi.

Bike (B)

29 miles
Warmup
- 2 mi @ RPEZ 3-4
Workout
- 26 mi @ RPEZ 4-5
Cooldown
- 1 mi @ RPEZ 2

70 miles
Warmup
- 2 mi @ RPEZ 2-3
Workout
- 68 mi @ RPEZ 4-5

Transition to run
- 4 mi @ RPEZ 3-4

Run (R)

6 miles
Warmup
- 0.5 mi @ RPEZ 2-3
Workout
- 5.25 mi @ RPEZ 5-6
Cooldown
- 0.25 mi @ RPEZ 2

14 miles
Warmup
- 0.5 mi @ RPEZ 2-3
Workout
- 13.25 mi @ RPEZ 4-5
Cooldown
- 0.25 mi @ RPEZ 2

Swim (S)

2,100 yds.
Warmup
- 2x100 freestyle
- 1x100 pull
- 2x50 kick

Workout
{15 sec rest between each of 10 sets}
- 3x200 freestyle
- 5x100 freestyle
- 2x100 pull
- 6x50 freestyle sprint

Cooldown
- 1x50 freestyle
- 1x50 choice

2,100 yds.
Warmup
- 2x100 freestyle
- 1x100 pull
- 2x50 kick

Workout
{15 sec rest between each of 12 sets}
- 2x300 freestyle
- 4x100 freestyle
- 3x100 pull
- 6x50 freestyle sprint

Cooldown
- 1x50 freestyle
- 1x50 choice

Weights (W)

Plyometric Circuit (PC)
Repeat 4x
- 10 box jumps
- 10 jump squats
- 10 jump lunges (each leg)
- 10 burpees
- 10 lateral bounds (each direction)
- Rest for 1 minute

Stability Ball Circuit (SBC)
Repeat 4x
- 10 dumbbell squats
- 10 dumbbell deadlifts
- 10 dumbbell lunges (each leg)
- 10 dumbbell step-ups (each leg)
- 10 calf raises
- Rest for 1 minute

Build Phase

Important Notes:

- ☐ At the end of your brick workout bike rides, pick up your cadence (RPMs), and keep your effort steady to prepare your legs for the run.
- ☐ It can be super easy to get sucked into comparing yourself to others. This sport is you vs. you. Don't let undermining thoughts demoralize you; keep your thoughts focused on the goal.

M	Tu	W	Th	F	Sa	Su
Rest	S - 2,100￼ W - KBC	B - 30 mi.	S - 2,100￼ W - RC	S - OW￼ R - 9 mi.	B - 73 mi.￼ R - 2 mi.	R - 15 mi.

Bike (B)

30 miles
Warmup
• 2 mi @ RPEZ 3-4
Workout
{Repeat 6x}
• 1 mi @ RPEZ 7-8
• 2 mi @ RPEZ 4-5

———
• 9 mi @ RPEZ 3-4
Cooldown
• 1 mi @ RPEZ 2

73 mile "brick"
Warmup
• 2 mi @ RPEZ 2-3
Workout
• 71 mi @ RPEZ 4-5

Transition to run
• 2 mi @ RPEZ 3-4

Swim (S)

2,100 yds.
Warmup
• 1x100 freestyle
• 4x50 choice
• 4x25 freestyle sprints

Workout
{15 sec rest between each of 12 sets}
• 2x400 freestyle
• 5x100 freestyle
• 4x50 choice
• 4x25 freestyle sprint

Cooldown
• 1x100 freestyle easy
• 1x100 choice

2,100 yds.
Warmup
• 1x100 freestyle
• 2x50 kick
• 1x100 pull

Workout
{20 sec rest between each of 12 sets}
• 2x400 freestyle
• 3x200 freestyle
• 2x100 pull
• 4x25 freestyle sprint

Cooldown
• 1x50 freestyle
• 1x50 choice

Run (R)

9 miles
Warmup
• 0.5 mi @ RPEZ 2-3
Workout
• 3.25 mi @ RPEZ 4-5

{Repeat 5x}
• 0.25 mi @ RPEZ 8-9
• 0.75 mi @ RPEZ 4-5
Cooldown
• 0.25 mi @ RPEZ 2

15 miles
Warmup
• 0.5 mi @ RPEZ 2-3
Workout
• 14.25 mi @ RPEZ 4-5
Cooldown
• 0.25 mi @ RPEZ 2

Weights (W)

Kettlebell Circuit (KBC)
Repeat 3-4x
• 10 kettlebell swings
• 10 goblet squats
• 10 kettlebell lunges (each leg)
• 20 single-arm kettlebell rows
• Rest for 1 minute

Resistance Circuit (RC)
Repeat 3-4x
• 10 resistance band squats
• 10 resistance band deadlifts
• 20 resistance band lateral walks
• 20 resistance band leg curls
• 10 resistance band glute bridges
• Rest for 1 minute

Week 28

Build Phase

Important Notes:

- ☐ Practice proper pacing during your long training sessions; remember–you're training for endurance, and embrace it.
- ☐ Find ways to mix in some variety: find a new route, find some new music, or do your strength workouts in a different location to change things up and stave off boredom.

M	Tu	W	Th	F	Sa	Su
Rest	S - 2,100 W - BWC	B - 26 mi. R - 6 mi.	S - 2,100 W - DLC	R - 6 mi.	B - 66 mi.	R - 13 mi.

Bike (B)

26 mile "brick"
Warmup
- 2 mi @ RPEZ 3-4

Workout
- 24 mi @ RPEZ 4-5

Transition to run
- 6 mi @ RPEZ 3-4

66 miles
Warmup
- 2 mi @ RPEZ 2-3

Workout
- 63 mi @ RPEZ 4-5

Cooldown
- 1 mi @ RPEZ 2

Run (R)

6 miles
Warmup
- 0.5 mi @ RPEZ 2-3

Workout
- 5.25 mi @ RPEZ 4-5

Cooldown
- 0.25 mi @ RPEZ 2

13 miles
Warmup
- 0.5 mi @ RPEZ 2-3

Workout
- 12.25 mi @ RPEZ 4-5

Cooldown
- 0.25 mi @ RPEZ 2

Swim (S)

2,100 yds.
Warmup
- 1x100 freestyle
- 1x100 pull
- 1x100 kick

Workout
{15 sec rest between each of 10 sets}
- 2x400 freestyle
- 5x100 freestyle
- 2x100 pull
- 4x50 freestyle down, choice back

Cooldown
- 1x50 freestyle
- 1x50 choice

2,100 yds.
Warmup
- 1x100 freestyle
- 1x100 pull
- 1x100 kick

Workout
{15 sec rest between each of 14 sets}
- 2x400 freestyle
- 4x100 freestyle
- 2x100 pull
- 6x50 freestyle down, choice back

Cooldown
- 1x50 freestyle
- 1x50 choice

Weights (W)

Bodyweight Circuit (BWC)
Repeat 3-4x
- 10 squats
- 20 single-leg lunges (10 each)
- 10 push-ups
- 20 mountain climbers
- 10 plank jacks
- Rest 1 min

Dumbbell Leg Circuit (DLC)
Repeat 3-4x
- 10 dumbbell squats
- 10 dumbbell deadlifts
- 10 dumbbell lunges (each leg)
- 10 dumbbell step-ups (each leg)
- 10 calf raises
- Rest for 1 minute

Week 29

Build Phase

Important Notes:

- Don't be satisfied with what works. Keep experimenting with different forms of fuel to find what works *best* for your body. What's just "good enough" for a 75-mile bike might not hold up under the strain of a full Ironman – use these workouts to figure this out.

| M | Tu | W | Th | F | Sa | Su |
| Rest | S - 2,100
W - PC | B - 31 mi. | S - 2,100
W - SBC | R - 6 mi. | B - 76 mi.
R - 5 mi. | R - 15 mi. |

Bike (B)

31 mile "brick"
Warmup
- 2 mi @ RPEZ 3-4
Workout
- 29 mi @ RPEZ 4-5

Transition to run
- 5 mi @ RPEZ 3-4

76 miles
Warmup
- 2 mi @ RPEZ 2-3
Workout
- 73 mi @ RPEZ 4-5
Cooldown
- 1 mi @ RPEZ 2

Run (R)

6 miles
Warmup
- 0.5 mi @ RPEZ 2-3
Workout
- 5.25 mi @ RPEZ 5-6
Cooldown
- 0.25 mi @ RPEZ 2

15 miles
Warmup
- 0.5 mi @ RPEZ 2-3
Workout
- 14.25 mi @ RPEZ 4-5
Cooldown
- 0.25 mi @ RPEZ 2

Swim (S)

2,100 yds.
Warmup
- 2x100 freestyle
- 1x100 pull
- 2x50 kick

Workout
{15 sec rest between each of 10 sets}
- 3x200 freestyle
- 5x100 freestyle
- 2x100 pull
- 6x50 freestyle sprint

Cooldown
- 1x50 freestyle
- 1x50 choice

2,100 yds.
Warmup
- 2x100 freestyle
- 1x100 pull
- 2x50 kick

Workout
{15 sec rest between each of 12 sets}
- 2x300 freestyle
- 4x100 freestyle
- 3x100 pull
- 6x50 freestyle sprint

Cooldown
- 1x50 freestyle
- 1x50 choice

Weights (W)

Plyometric Circuit (PC)
Repeat 4x
- 10 box jumps
- 10 jump squats
- 10 jump lunges (each leg)
- 10 burpees
- 10 lateral bounds (each direction)
- Rest for 1 minute

Stability Ball Circuit (SBC)
Repeat 4x
- 10 dumbbell squats
- 10 dumbbell deadlifts
- 10 dumbbell lunges (each leg)
- 10 dumbbell step-ups (each leg)
- 10 calf raises
- Rest for 1 minute

Week 30
Build Phase

Important Notes:

- ☐ Recovery tools, like a foam roller, massage gun, or even a simple lacrosse ball can be massively helpful in releasing tight, sore muscles.
- ☐ Incorporate hill training in your shorter bikes and runs to build strength and improve your overall fitness.

M	Tu	W	Th	F	Sa	Su
Rest	S - 2,100 W - KBC	B - 30 mi. R - 4 mi.	S - 2,100 W - RC	S - OW R - 9 mi.	B - 79 mi. R - 4 mi.	R - 15 mi.

Bike (B)

32 miles
Warmup
• 2 mi @ RPEZ 3-4
Workout
• 30 mi @ RPEZ 4-5

Transition to run
• 4 mi @ RPEZ 3-4

79 mile "brick"
Warmup
• 2 mi @ RPEZ 2-3
Workout
• 77 mi @ RPEZ 4-5

Transition to run
• 2 mi @ RPEZ 3-4

Run (R)

8 miles
Warmup
• 0.5 mi @ RPEZ 2-3
Workout
• 2.25 mi @ RPEZ 4-5

{Repeat 5x}
• 0.25 mi @ RPEZ 8-9
• 0.75 mi @ RPEZ 4-5
Cooldown
• 0.25 mi @ RPEZ 2

15 miles
Warmup
• 0.5 mi @ RPEZ 2-3
Workout
• 14.25 mi @ RPEZ 4-5
Cooldown
• 0.25 mi @ RPEZ 2

Swim (S)

2,100 yds.
Warmup
• 1x100 freestyle
• 4x50 choice
• 4x25 freestyle sprints

Workout
{15 sec rest between each of 12 sets}
• 2x400 freestyle
• 5x100 freestyle
• 4x50 choice
• 4x25 freestyle sprint

Cooldown
• 1x100 freestyle easy
• 1x100 choice

2,100 yds.
Warmup
• 1x100 freestyle
• 2x50 kick
• 1x100 pull

Workout
{20 sec rest between each of 12 sets}
• 2x400 freestyle
• 6x100 freestyle
• 2x100 pull
• 4x25 freestyle sprint

Cooldown
• 1x50 freestyle
• 1x50 choice

Weights (W)

Kettlebell Circuit (KBC)
Repeat 3-4x
• 10 kettlebell swings
• 10 goblet squats
• 10 kettlebell lunges (each leg)
• 20 single-arm kettlebell rows
• Rest for 1 minute

Resistance Circuit (RC)
Repeat 3-4x
• 10 resistance band squats
• 10 resistance band deadlifts
• 20 resistance band lateral walks
• 20 resistance band leg curls
• 10 resistance band glute bridges
• Rest for 1 minute

"Perseverance is the hard work you do after you get tired of doing the hard work you already did."

Newt Gingrich

Week 31

Peak Phase

Welcome to The Peak Phase. This seven-week period contains the longest endurance workouts we'll do in training.

Important Notes:

☐ Struggling to find room for all the fuel you've got on your bike? Look into a bento box – you can store a good amount of fuel in those puppies, freeing up your race kit from being stuffed full.

M	Tu	W	Th	F	Sa	Su
Rest	S - 2,100 W - BWC	B - 32 mi. R - 4 mi.	S - 2,100 W - DLC	R - 4 mi.	B - 82 mi.	R - 16 mi.

Bike (B)

32 mile "brick"
Warmup
• 2 mi @ RPEZ 3-4
Workout
• 30 mi @ RPEZ 4-5

Transition to run
• 4 mi @ RPEZ 3-4

82 miles
Warmup
• 2 mi @ RPEZ 2-3
Workout
• 79 mi @ RPEZ 4-5
Cooldown
• 1 mi @ RPEZ 2

Run (R)

4 miles
Warmup
• 0.5 mi @ RPEZ 2-3
Workout
• 3.25 mi @ RPEZ 4-5
Cooldown
• 0.25 mi @ RPEZ 2

16 miles
Warmup
• 0.5 mi @ RPEZ 2-3
Workout
• 15.25 mi @ RPEZ 4-5
Cooldown
• 0.25 mi @ RPEZ 2

Peak Phase

Ironman
App

Important Notes:

- ☐ Download the Ironman app, and share it with your cheering team; they'll be able to track you in real time as you make your way to the finish.
- ☐ Lube is your friend for these long workouts: toes, armpits, crotch, and between your glutes.

M	Tu	W	Th	F	Sa	Su
Rest	S - 2,100 W - PC	B - 29 mi. R - 6 mi.	S - 2,100 W - SBC	R - 8 mi.	B - 74 mi.	R - 15 mi.

Bike (B)

29 mile "brick"
Warmup
• 2 mi @ RPEZ 3-4
Workout
• 27 mi @ RPEZ 4-5

Transition to run
• 6 mi @ RPEZ 3-4

74 miles
Warmup
• 2 mi @ RPEZ 2-3
Workout
• 71 mi @ RPEZ 4-5
Cooldown
• 1 mi @ RPEZ 2

Run (R)

8 miles
Warmup
• 0.5 mi @ RPEZ 2-3
Workout
• 7.25 mi @ RPEZ 5-6
Cooldown
• 0.25 mi @ RPEZ 2

15 miles
Warmup
• 0.5 mi @ RPEZ 2-3
Workout
• 14.25 mi @ RPEZ 4-5
Cooldown
• 0.25 mi @ RPEZ 2

Swim (S)

2,100 yds.
Warmup
• 2x100 freestyle
• 1x100 pull
• 2x50 kick

Workout
{15 sec rest between each of 10 sets}
• 3x200 freestyle
• 5x100 freestyle
• 2x100 pull
• 6x50 freestyle sprint

Cooldown
• 1x50 freestyle
• 1x50 choice

2,100 yds.
Warmup
• 2x100 freestyle
• 1x100 pull
• 2x50 kick

Workout
{15 sec rest between each of 12 sets}
• 2x300 freestyle
• 4x100 freestyle
• 3x100 pull
• 6x50 freestyle sprint

Cooldown
• 1x50 freestyle
• 1x50 choice

Weights (W)

Plyometric Circuit (PC)
Repeat 4x
• 10 box jumps
• 10 jump squats
• 10 jump lunges (each leg)
• 10 burpees
• 10 lateral bounds (each direction)
• Rest for 1 minute

Stability Ball Circuit (SBC)
Repeat 4x
• 10 dumbbell squats
• 10 dumbbell deadlifts
• 10 dumbbell lunges (each leg)
• 10 dumbbell step-ups (each leg)
• 10 calf raises
• Rest for 1 minute

Week 33

Peak Phase

Important Notes:

☐ There's a saying in Ironman: "nothing new on race day." By now, hopefully, you've got a plan for what you'll wear on race day. Practice in it – at least a couple times, and make sure it's going to work for you. You're going to find out; better to find out now.

M	Tu	W	Th	F	Sa	Su
Rest	S - 2,100 W - KBC	B - 34 mi. R - 6 mi.	S - 2,100 W - RC	S - OW R - 9 mi.	B - 85 mi.	R - 17 mi.

Bike (B)

34 miles
Warmup
• 2 mi @ RPEZ 3-4
Workout
• 32 mi @ RPEZ 4-5

Transition to run
• 6 mi @ RPEZ 3-4

85 miles
Warmup
• 2 mi @ RPEZ 2-3
Workout
• 82 mi @ RPEZ 4-5
Cooldown
• 1 mi @ RPEZ 2

Run (R)

7 miles
Warmup
• 0.5 mi @ RPEZ 2-3
Workout
• 2.25 mi @ RPEZ 4-5

{Repeat 4x}
• 0.25 mi @ RPEZ 8-9
• 0.75 mi @ RPEZ 4-5
Cooldown
• 0.25 mi @ RPEZ 2

17 miles
Warmup
• 0.5 mi @ RPEZ 2-3
Workout
• 16.25 mi @ RPEZ 4-5
Cooldown
• 0.25 mi @ RPEZ 2

Swim (S)

2,100 yds.
Warmup
• 1x100 freestyle
• 4x50 choice
• 4x25 freestyle sprints

Workout
{15 sec rest between each of 12 sets}
• 2x400 freestyle
• 5x100 freestyle
• 4x50 choice
• 4x25 freestyle sprint

Cooldown
• 1x100 freestyle easy
• 1x100 choice

2,100 yds.
Warmup
• 2x100 freestyle
• 2x50 kick
• 1x100 pull

Workout
{20 sec rest between each of 12 sets}
• 2x400 freestyle
• 5x100 freestyle
• 2x100 pull
• 4x25 freestyle sprint

Cooldown
• 1x50 freestyle
• 1x50 choice

Weights (W)

Kettlebell Circuit (KBC)
Repeat 3-4x
• 10 kettlebell swings
• 10 goblet squats
• 10 kettlebell lunges (each leg)
• 20 single-arm kettlebell rows
• Rest for 1 minute

Resistance Circuit (RC)
Repeat 3-4x
• 10 resistance band squats
• 10 resistance band deadlifts
• 20 resistance band lateral walks
• 20 resistance band leg curls
• 10 resistance band glute bridges
• Rest for 1 minute

Week 34
Peak Phase

Important Notes:

☐ These long bike rides and runs will really put your nutrition plan to the test. By now you should have a good idea of your sweat rates, and as a result your required water intake. If you're still tinkering, don't worry. Still plenty of workouts to figure it out. Just keep testing to find what works best for your body.

M	Tu	W	Th	F	Sa	Su
Rest	S - 2,100 W - BWC	B - 34 mi. R - 5 mi.	S - 2,100 W - DLC	R - 8 mi.	B - 88 mi.	R - 16 mi.

Bike (B)

34 mile "brick"
Warmup
• 2 mi @ RPEZ 3-4
Workout
• 32 mi @ RPEZ 4-5

Transition to run
• 5 mi @ RPEZ 3-4

88 miles
Warmup
• 2 mi @ RPEZ 2-3
Workout
• 85 mi @ RPEZ 4-5
Cooldown
• 1 mi @ RPEZ 2

Run (R)

8 miles
Warmup
• 0.5 mi @ RPEZ 2-3
Workout
• 7.25 mi @ RPEZ 4-5
Cooldown
• 0.25 mi @ RPEZ 2

16 miles
Warmup
• 0.5 mi @ RPEZ 2-3
Workout
• 15.25 mi @ RPEZ 4-5
Cooldown
• 0.25 mi @ RPEZ 2

Swim (S)

2,100 yds.
Warmup
• 1x100 freestyle
• 1x100 pull
• 1x100 kick

Workout
{15 sec rest between each of 10 sets}
• 2x400 freestyle
• 5x100 freestyle
• 2x100 pull
• 4x50 freestyle down, choice back

Cooldown
• 1x50 freestyle
• 1x50 choice

2,100 yds.
Warmup
• 1x100 freestyle
• 1x100 pull
• 1x100 kick

Workout
{15 sec rest between each of 14 sets}
• 2x400 freestyle
• 4x100 freestyle
• 2x100 pull
• 6x50 freestyle down, choice back

Cooldown
• 1x50 freestyle
• 1x50 choice

Weights (W)

Bodyweight Circuit (BWC)
Repeat 3-4x
• 10 squats
• 20 single-leg lunges (10 each)
• 10 push-ups
• 20 mountain climbers
• 10 plank jacks
• Rest 1 min

Dumbbell Leg Circuit (DLC)
Repeat 3-4x
• 10 dumbbell squats
• 10 dumbbell deadlifts
• 10 dumbbell lunges (each leg)
• 10 dumbbell step-ups (each leg)
• 10 calf raises
• Rest for 1 minute

Week 35

Peak Phase

Important Notes:

☐ Just a few weeks out from the race; now would be a good time to bring your bike into the shop for a tuneup. Let them know you're training for an Ironman in a few weeks and they'll usually be able to expedite service, and get it back to you so you don't miss a workout.

M	Tu	W	Th	F	Sa	Su
Rest	S - 2,100 W - PC	B - 36 mi.	S - 2,100 W - SBC	R - 9 mi.	B - 90 mi.	R - 15 mi.

Bike (B)

36 miles
Warmup
• 2 mi @ RPEZ 3-4
Workout
• 33 mi @ RPEZ 4-5
Cooldown
• 1 mi @ RPEZ 2

90 miles
Warmup
• 2 mi @ RPEZ 2-3
Workout
• 87 mi @ RPEZ 4-5
Cooldown
• 1 mi @ RPEZ 2

Run (R)

9 miles
Warmup
• 0.5 mi @ RPEZ 2-3
Workout
• 8.25 mi @ RPEZ 5-6
Cooldown
• 0.25 mi @ RPEZ 2

15 miles
Warmup
• 0.5 mi @ RPEZ 2-3
Workout
• 14.25 mi @ RPEZ 4-5
Cooldown
• 0.25 mi @ RPEZ 2

Peak Phase

Important Notes:

- ☐ Hundred mile bike this week. Download an audio book. You're in for a long sit.
- ☐ Last open-water swim before the Ironman; make it a good one. Shoot for 3,000 yards of nice, easy swimming. Think of this as a dry run for the Ironman, and go through the warmup routine you plan to use at the race.

M	Tu	W	Th	F	Sa	Su
Rest	S - 2,100 W - KBC	B - 29 mi. R - 6 mi.	S - 2,100 W - RC	S - OW R - 7 mi.	B - 100 mi.	R - 12 mi.

Bike (B)

29 miles
Warmup
• 2 mi @ RPEZ 3-4
Workout
• 27 mi @ RPEZ 4-5

Transition to run
• 6 mi @ RPEZ 3-4

100 miles
Warmup
• 2 mi @ RPEZ 2-3
Workout
• 97 mi @ RPEZ 4-5
Cooldown
• 1 mi @ RPEZ 2

Run (R)

7 miles
Warmup
• 0.5 mi @ RPEZ 2-3
Workout
• 6.25 mi @ RPEZ 4-5
Cooldown
• 0.25 mi @ RPEZ 2

12 miles
Warmup
• 0.5 mi @ RPEZ 2-3
Workout
• 11.25 mi @ RPEZ 4-5
Cooldown
• 0.25 mi @ RPEZ 2

Swim (S)

2,100 yds.
Warmup
• 1x100 freestyle
• 4x50 choice
• 4x25 freestyle sprints

Workout
{15 sec rest between each of 12 sets}
• 2x400 freestyle
• 5x100 freestyle
• 4x50 choice
• 4x25 freestyle sprint

Cooldown
• 1x100 freestyle easy
• 1x100 choice

2,100 yds.
Warmup
• 1x100 freestyle
• 2x50 kick
• 1x100 pull

Workout
{20 sec rest between each of 12 sets}
• 2x400 freestyle
• 5x100 freestyle
• 2x100 pull
• 8x25 freestyle sprint

Cooldown
• 1x50 freestyle
• 1x50 choice

Weights (W)

Kettlebell Circuit (KBC)
Repeat 3-4x
• 10 kettlebell swings
• 10 goblet squats
• 10 kettlebell lunges (each leg)
• 20 single-arm kettlebell rows
• Rest for 1 minute

Resistance Circuit (RC)
Repeat 3-4x
• 10 resistance band squats
• 10 resistance band deadlifts
• 20 resistance band lateral walks
• 20 resistance band leg curls
• 10 resistance band glute bridges
• Rest for 1 minute

Week 37

Peak Phase

Important Notes:

- ☐ Book a reservation for your pre-race dinner (carb loading the night prior); don't wait or the good restaurants will book up.
- ☐ You'll do your longest run this week. Make sure you've got a fuel plan, and a means to make it happen. If you need to, you can always set fuel out in front of your house and do loops past.

M	Tu	W	Th	F	Sa	Su
Rest	S - 2,100 W - BWC	B - 31 mi.	S - 2,100 W - DLC	R - 7 mi.	B - 73 mi. R - 6 mi.	R - 18 mi.

Bike (B)

31 miles
Warmup
• 2 mi @ RPEZ 3-4
Workout
• 28 mi @ RPEZ 4-5
Cooldown
• 1 mi @ RPEZ 2

73 mile "brick"
Warmup
• 2 mi @ RPEZ 2-3
Workout
• 71 mi @ RPEZ 4-5

Transition to run
• 6 mi @ RPEZ 3-4

Run (R)

7 miles
Warmup
• 0.5 mi @ RPEZ 2-3
Workout
• 6.25 mi @ RPEZ 4-5
Cooldown
• 0.25 mi @ RPEZ 2

18 miles
Warmup
• 0.5 mi @ RPEZ 2-3
Workout
• 17.25 mi @ RPEZ 4-5
Cooldown
• 0.25 mi @ RPEZ 2

work, perseverance, learning, studying, sacrifice and most of all, love of what you are doing or learning to do."

Pele

Week 38
Taper Phase

Important Notes:

☐   We're in the taper phase now; workout intensity and volumes will drop off big time. You've done the hard work to build up your endurance; now it's time to let your body recover so you can be ready to give it your all on race day.

M	Tu	W	Th	F	Sa	Su
Rest	S - 2,100	B - 21 mi.	S - 2,100	R - 3 mi.	B - 40 mi.	R - 11 mi.

Bike (B)

21 miles
Warmup
• 2 mi @ RPEZ 3-4
Workout
• 18 mi @ RPEZ 4-5
Cooldown
• 1 mi @ RPEZ 2

40 miles
Warmup
• 2 mi @ RPEZ 2-3
Workout
• 37 mi @ RPEZ 4-5
Cooldown
• 1 mi @ RPEZ 2

Run (R)

3 miles
Warmup
• 0.5 mi @ RPEZ 2-3
Workout
• 2.25 mi @ RPEZ 5-6
Cooldown
• 0.25 mi @ RPEZ 2

11 miles
Warmup
• 0.5 mi @ RPEZ 2-3
Workout
• 10.25 mi @ RPEZ 4-5
Cooldown
• 0.25 mi @ RPEZ 2

Swim (S)

2,100 yds.
Warmup
• 2x100 freestyle
• 1x100 pull
• 2x50 kick

Workout
{15 sec rest between each of 10 sets}
• 3x200 freestyle
• 5x100 freestyle
• 2x100 pull
• 6x50 freestyle sprint

Cooldown
• 1x50 freestyle
• 1x50 choice

1,500 yds.
Warmup
• 2x100 freestyle
• 1x100 pull
• 2x50 kick

Workout
{15 sec rest between each of 12 sets}
• 1x300 freestyle
• 2x100 freestyle
• 3x100 pull
• 4x50 freestyle sprint

Cooldown
• 1x50 freestyle
• 1x50 choice

Taper Phase

Important Notes:

☐ Race week; time to refresh yourself on the logistics (page 82).
☐ When you get to the race, don't get overwhelmed by the fancy bikes – you've done the work; you deserve to be here, and you're ready.

M	Tu	W	Th	F	Sa	Su
Rest	S - 1,000	B - 10 mi.	Rest	R - 3 mi.	Rest	**Race**

Bike (B)

10 miles
Warmup
• 2 mi @ RPEZ 3-4
Workout
• 7 mi @ RPEZ 4-5
Cooldown
• 1 mi @ RPEZ 2

Run (R)

3 miles
Warmup
• 0.5 mi @ RPEZ 2-3
Workout
• 2.25 mi @ RPEZ 5-6
Cooldown
• 0.25 mi @ RPEZ 2

Swim (S)

1,000 yds.
Warmup
• 2x100 freestyle
• 1x100 pull
• 2x50 kick

Workout
{15 sec rest between each of 10 sets}
• 3x100 freestyle
• 2x100 pull

Cooldown
• 1x50 freestyle
• 1x50 choice

LOG
IST
ICS

LOGISTICS

The final piece of a well-prepared Ironman plan is logistics. We'll break logistics down into a few parts:

- Timeline
- Packing
- Packing Checklist
- Transition Bags
- Pre-Race
- Race-Day

Timeline

Several months before the race, you'll receive an email outlining the day-by-day schedule. The timeline below is generally true, and helps outline what you need to do when, but make sure to check your event schedule.

2-3 days before the race: pack your gear. If you're flying to the race, it's best to leave some buffer for delays and travel three days prior to race day.

2 days before the race: two days prior to race day is when most athletes will arrive at the race location.

When you arrive, drop your bags and gear at your hotel, and make your way to the athletes village where you can check out the transition areas, see the swim layout, and shop the Ironman store.

1-2 days before the race: you'll need to complete two administrative tasks in the day or two before the race:

1. Check-in
2. Attend an athlete briefing

Savvy athletes may also choose to drive the bike route, so they can familiarize themselves with the course.

1 day before the race: the day prior to the race, you'll need to:

1. Set up your bike in T1
2. Drop off your T2 bag
3. Pick up your timing chip

Your bike will stay in T1 overnight. You will be able to access your bike about three hours before the race start on the morning of the race (to do last-minute tweaks, and fill water bottles).

The night before the race, set out all of your necessities in your hotel room for the following morning.

Race Day: Eat a complex-carb-rich breakfast (oatmeal is a classic) first thing in the morning (to give yourself some time to digest before the race start).

Then get dressed in your tri suit, secure your race chip to your ankle, and put your race number tattoos on your body (one set the outside of your upper arm, and one set on the outside of your lower leg).

Pack all your swim gear in a backpack, and put on some clothes over the top of your tri suit that will keep you comfortable.

When you arrive, you'll first go to your bike to top off your tires, put your water bottles on your bike, and do a final systems check.

Once your bike is ready for the day, you'll make your way to the swim start to dress for the swim.

The swim start area will be crowded, and hectic – put on headphones and some calming music to drown out the noise, and sip on a simple carb source, like a sports drink.

About 40 min. before the swim start (usually at 7:00a) you should put your street clothes in your bag, and get dressed for the swim.

Once you're dressed, make your way to the designated swim warm up area. The main goal here is to acclimate to the water temperature. One of the most common reasons athletes drop out of the race is because they fail to acclimate to the cold water, and experience cold-water diaphragmatic seizures – the reactionary "gasping" that happens when you get into cold water. That reaction spirals into panicked breathing, and defeating thoughts that cause athletes to tap out.

Don't fall into that trap.

Once you're feeling comfortable in the water, make your way out, and to the queue of athletes at the swim start.

At the swim start you'll see a descending order of swim times (shown as the amount of time it takes you to swim 100 yards at a comfortable pace) ranging from the fastest swimmers at the front, to the slowest at the back.

Find the time group that you think you'll swim with (most athletes will be around 2:00), and make your way to the back of that group (it's easier to swim past people than to have people swimming past – or over – you.

The race will start with The National Anthem, and a gun start.

Afterwards athletes will start being allowed to start in pairs or triplets in what's called a "staggered start."

Once you're at the front of the line, race officials will tell your pair when to enter the water.

Packing

Between bike, run, swim, nutrition, and all the food, pre-and-post-race accoutrements, and clothing, there's a lot of planning that goes into packing for a race.

Our best advice: do a step-by-step walkthrough of the raceday timeline, and literally dress yourself in – or outfit your bike with – all of the gear you plan to use:

Sleep: bring your favorite pillow, blanket, and PJs – whatever will make you feel comfortable, and help you get rest the night before the race.

Pre-Race Meal: don't count on finding the foods you got used to eating during training.. Pack your tried-and-true pre-race fuels, and make sure you've got them ready now.

Pre-Race Prep: put on your tri suit, put your hands on your body-marking tattoos (or marker), smart watch, sunscreen – all of the items you plan to put on and keep on all day.

Start Line: put on the clothes you plan to wear over your tri suit on the morning of the race. Add a pair of flip flops. Take your pre-race outfit off, and set it aside.

Swim: put on your wetsuit, swim cap, and goggles. Put in your ear plugs. Got everything you'd need to hop in the water? Good. Now take it off, and set it aside.

Bike: get your bike all set up for a 112mi. ride. Put all the fuel you plan to carry on your bike – make sure it fits. If you're planning to attach things to your bike frame, make sure you've got a means to do so – put your hands on the tape or zip ties you plan to use, and the scissors you'll need to cut them.

Once your bike is all set, get yourself dressed for a bike: socks, shoes, glasses, helmet, gloves – everything.

Once you feel confident you've got it all, take it off, set it in a pile, and change into your run gear.

Run: put on your run socks (if you plan to change), find your baby powder or toe lube, put on your race belt, hat, and sunglasses.

Ready to run? Great. Now take it off and put it in a pile.

Finish Line: when you get to the finish line you'll be chaffed, sore, and tired. Pack your most comfortable sandals, sweatshirt, shorts, and sweatpants.

Pack some ibuprofen, acetaminophen, bandages (for blisters), chapstick, a pack of baby wipes (to wipe the salt crystals off your body), and a garbage bag (to keep your wet/dirty race clothes separate from the rest of your stuff in your bag).

PACK CHECKLIST

Swim

- ☐ Wetsuit
- ☐ Goggles (2 sets)
- ☐ Swim Cap (2)
- ☐ Vaseline or Body Glide
- ☐ Open-Water Buoy
- ☐ Ear plugs*
- ☐ _____
- ☐ _____
- ☐ _____

Bike

- ☐ Bike
- ☐ Helmet
- ☐ Bike shoes
- ☐ Water Bottles
- ☐ Bike Pump
- ☐ Spare tire tubes
- ☐ CO2 + CO2 cartridges
- ☐ Quick Pump
- ☐ Cycling gloves*
- ☐ Bento box / On-bike fuel storage
- ☐ Saddle bag
- ☐ _____
- ☐ _____
- ☐ _____

Fuel +

- ☐ Pre-race meal
- ☐ Race fuel solids + liquids
- ☐ Acetaminophen & Ibuprofen
- ☐ Blister bandages
- ☐ Foam roller
- ☐ Chapstick
- ☐ _____
- ☐ _____
- ☐ _____

Run

- ☐ Shoes
- ☐ Race Belt
- ☐ Socks
- ☐ _____
- ☐ _____
- ☐ _____

Clothing

- ☐ Tri suit
- ☐ Running hat
- ☐ Sunglasses (2 pair)
- ☐ Running shorts
- ☐ Flip flops
- ☐ Fitness watch + charger
- ☐ Phone charger
- ☐ _____
- ☐ _____
- ☐ _____
- ☐ _____
- ☐ _____
- ☐ _____

Miscellaneous

- ☐ Sunscreen
- ☐ Baby wipes
- ☐ Plastic grocery bag
- ☐ Rubber bands
- ☐ Electrical tape
- ☐ Scissors
- ☐ Zip ties
- ☐ Baby powder
- ☐ Stick-on tattoo race numbers
- ☐ Bike multi tools
- ☐ Towels (2)
- ☐ Foam roller
- ☐ Distinctive bag markings
- ☐ _____

Transition Bags

Unlike shorter races, which usually allow you to stash your stuff on a towel under your bike rack, Ironman races don't typically allow athletes to store their gear in transition. Instead, they distribute Ironman bags: five in total, each of which are marked with your race number.

Ironman Bag 1: Dry Clothes - this bag serves double duty; it'll carry your swim start stuff (and any last-minute bike service items) to the swim start (and T1 area). There's no requirement that you use the provided plastic bag; feel free to use the backpack you receive in your race welcome kit.

After you've prepped your bike, put your warm pre-race clothes in this bag, and send it off with your cheering squad – you'll be happy to have warm, dry clothes when you reach the finish.

Pro tip: you'll be totally fine without a bike pump; hundreds of other folks will have one that they'll be happy to lend.

Pro tip: put any post-race comfort items in this same bag, so you can have them at the finish line: ibuprofen, acetaminophen, bandages (for blisters and chafes, which you'll have many), chapstick, and anything else that will help you start the recovery process post-race.

Ironman Bag 2: Swim to Bike - your swim-to-bike bag should have all your bike essentials that aren't already attached to your bike – including your socks, bike shoes, helmet, sunglasses, and any other items you want to have with you on the bike.

If you didn't already stash them on your bike, this bag should also contain things like your solid fuels, sunscreen, chamois cream, salt tablets, extra electrolyte powder or tablets, spare tube, tire lever, and CO_2.

Pro tip: Don't put things like water bottles in this bag; anything that you can attach to your bike should already have been attached before the race starts (hint: here's where you put that electrical tape to use to attach sunglasses, and fuel).

Ironman Bag 3: Bike Special Needs

This bag is designed to hold the things you hope you'll never need, and fully plan to never see again (these bags aren't returned to athletes after the race).

But if things go wrong, this bag will be your emergency stash. Pack single-use sunscreen and chamois cream packets, pain relievers, anti-diarrheal medication, and contact lens solution, if needed. You can also include extra bottles of electrolyte powder or tablets, gels, chews, bars, and a spare tube with CO_2.

Ironman Bag 3: Bike Special Needs (Continued) - Remember not to add anything new on race day; 50 miles into the bike is not a good time to discover you're allergic to an ingredient in the free sunscreen you picked up at athletes village.

Ironman Bag 4: Bike to Run - after you reach the bike dismount line, volunteers will guide you to the final staging area where you'll pick up your bike-to-run transition bag. Make sure to have your run shoes, socks, a change of clothes (if you plan to do so), your race belt (already sized to fit you) with your number and any fuel already attached, a hat/visor, sunscreen, and anti-chafe stick or cream.

Pro tip: most athletes will finish their after the sun has set. Consider using a hat and sunglasses that you don't mind parting with – it can be a relief to ditch these late in the race.

Ironman Bag 5: Run Special Needs
The run special needs bag should contain everything you need to finish strong. As always, pack single-use sunscreen and chamois cream packets, pain relievers, anti-diarrheal medication, and contact lens solution, if needed. Make sure to stick to your fueling plan and only pack extra food if necessary.

Pro tip: your bag will be one of hundreds – if not more than a thousand - visually identical bags; make yours stand out with some ribbon or bright tape, so you can quickly find it.

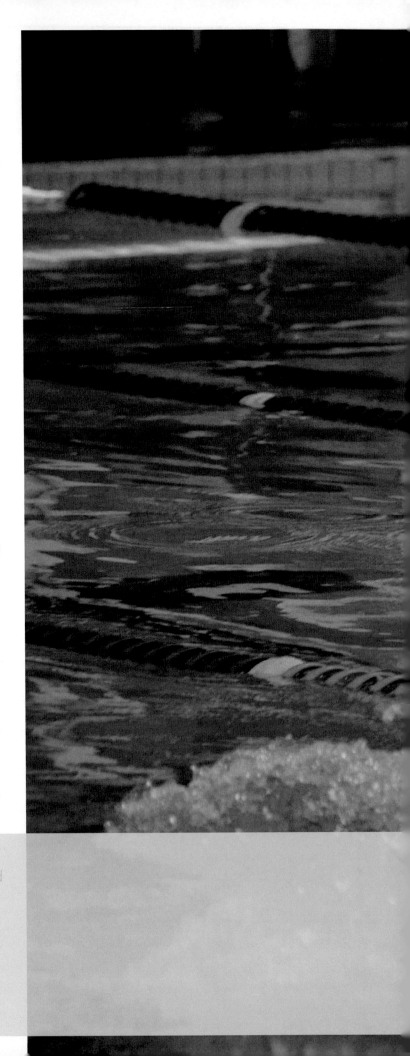

Pre-Race

Traveling to an Ironman race present some unique logistics challenges – mainly: "how do I transport my bike?"

Depending on how you're planning to travel (by ground or air), there's a range of options.

If you plan to drive, you can use a bike transport attached to your car's hitch, or disassemble your bike and store it in the back of a SUV or truck.

If you plan to fly, however, you've gotta figure out how you're going to ensure your bike arrives to your destination without being damaged.

In general, you've got two options:
1. You can pay for services, like <u>TriBike Transport</u>, which will pick up your bike and transport it to the race location
2. You can transport the bike in a bike case.

Athletes that fly to the race location use a pretty even mix of the two options; it's a matter of personal preference.

If you choose option two; to transport the bike with you on your flight you can choose either to buy a bike case or rent one (much cheaper for most who would only ever infrequently use this tool).

Contact your local bike shop; they likely have a rental program, or may be able to refer you to a shop that does.

Pre-Race Planning

If you've got a cheering team coming with you to watch the race and celebrate your accomplishment, you'll want to cover off on a few logistics before the race starts:
1. Where are we going to meet after the race, and
2. Who is going to pick up my transition bags and bike?

Where to Meet?
The race finish will be incredibly crowded and loud. Trying to find your cheering team amidst all the commotion can be challenging if you don't agree on a good place to meet after you've finished the race.

In the day or two prior, scope out the finish area, and pick a prominent landmark that's more than 100yds away from the finish line; tell your cheering team you'll meet them there after you finish.

Who is getting my stuff?
On the list of things you could conceivably want to do after you finish the race, walking will be at or near the bottom.

You can certainly go pick up your bike and all your bags after you finish, but if you've got a willing member of your cheering team, you can save yourself the effort and give one of those cheerers one of your bike pick up tickets (which you'll get in your check-in packet). They can use that ticket to pickup your bike, T1, and T2 bags.

Race Day

If you've trained exclusively with headphones and music so far, I'm sorry to tell you, but you won't be able to use them during the race.

In the name of athlete safety, you are not allowed to use headphones or communication devices of any kind.

But don't worry about it. There will be plenty to keep your mind busy, and lots of spectators to cheer you along – you honestly won't miss them.

Drafting

Drafting is the practice of following another athlete closely enough that they create a "wake" either in the air or water.

Drafting can save significant energy, and help you go faster, but it's not legal everywhere.

You can draft during the swim and the run.

You cannot draft on the bike.

Ironman defines drafting on the bike as following within 12 meters of the front of another bike (less than about six bike lengths of clear space).

You are allowed to "draft" as Ironman has defined it only when you're passing a bike in front of you, but don't linger; you can only be in the "drafting zone" for a maximum of 25 seconds.

Blocking

While biking, athletes must ride single file on the far-right side (or left side depending on local law) of the bike course road except when passing another athlete.

Number Bib

You are not required to wear your bib during the swim or bike.

But you do need to wear your bib numbers while running, and you're required to have the numbers displayed on the front of your body.

Fuel Stations

You'll find fuel stations every 20 miles or so on the bike, and every 1.5-2 miles on the run.

You're free to stop entirely, or move through these at your discretion. Grab the fuel that you need, and discard any empty fuel containers/wrappers there.

Don't discard trash outside of the designated drop areas (at fuel stations), or you could get a time penalty.

Pro tip: use your fuel plan to figure out how much fuel (and what kind) to gather from these stations; don't just wing it – <u>nothing new on race day.</u>

THIS IS POSSI-BLE

Whatever it was that you set out to prove, you've already accomplished it.

Race day is just a ceremony to celebrate it.

You're capable. You're ready. You deserve this. Now go do it.

Made in the USA
Las Vegas, NV
14 December 2024

14372842R00059